Constitutional Law

Third Edition

2009 Supplement

ASPEN PUBLISHERS

2009 Supplement

Constitutional Law

Third Edition

Erwin Chemerinsky
Dean and Distinguished Professor of Law
University of California, Irvine, School of Law

Wolters Kluwer
Law & Business

AUSTIN   BOSTON   CHICAGO   NEW YORK   THE NETHERLANDS

Aspen Publishers
Attn: Permissions Department
76 Ninth Avenue, 7th Floor
New York, NY 10011-5201

To contact Customer Care, e-mail customer.care@aspenpublishers.com, call 1-800-234-1660, fax 1-800-901-9075, or mail correspondence to:

Aspen Publishers
Attn: Order Department
PO Box 990
Frederick, MD 21705

Printed in the United States of America.

1 2 3 4 5 6 7 8 9 0

ISBN 978-0-7355-8234-7

Library of Congress Cataloging-in-Publication Data

Chemerinsky, Erwin.
    Constitutional law/Erwin Chemerinsky.—3rd ed.
        p. cm.
    Includes bibliographical references and index.
    ISBN 978-0-7355-7717-6 (casebook)
    ISBN 978-0-7355-8234-7 (supplement)
    1. Constitutional law—United States—Cases. I. Title.

    KF4549.C44 2009
    342.73—dc22

                                                                2009008261

About Wolters Kluwer Law & Business

Wolters Kluwer Law & Business is a leading provider of research information and workflow solutions in key specialty areas. The strengths of the individual brands of Aspen Publishers, CCH, Kluwer Law International and Loislaw are aligned within Wolters Kluwer Law & Business to provide comprehensive, in-depth solutions and expert-authored content for the legal, professional and education markets.

CCH was founded in 1913 and has served more than four generations of business professionals and their clients. The CCH products in the Wolters Kluwer Law & Business group are highly regarded electronic and print resources for legal, securities, antitrust and trade regulation, government contracting, banking, pension, payroll, employment and labor, and healthcare reimbursement and compliance professionals.

Aspen Publishers is a leading information provider for attorneys, business professionals and law students. Written by preeminent authorities, Aspen products offer analytical and practical information in a range of specialty practice areas from securities law and intellectual property to mergers and acquisitions and pension/benefits. Aspen's trusted legal education resources provide professors and students with high-quality, up-to-date and effective resources for successful instruction and study in all areas of the law.

Kluwer Law International supplies the global business community with comprehensive English-language international legal information. Legal practitioners, corporate counsel and business executives around the world rely on the Kluwer Law International journals, loose-leafs, books and electronic products for authoritative information in many areas of international legal practice.

Loislaw is a premier provider of digitized legal content to small law firm practitioners of various specializations. Loislaw provides attorneys with the ability to quickly and efficiently find the necessary legal information they need, when and where they need it, by facilitating access to primary law as well as state-specific law, records, forms and treatises.

Wolters Kluwer Law & Business, a unit of Wolters Kluwer, is headquartered in New York and Riverwoods, Illinois. Wolters Kluwer is a leading multinational publisher and information services company.

Contents

Preface

The third edition of *Constitutional Law* was published in the spring of 2009 and is complete through the end of October Term 2007, which ended on June 26, 2008. This supplement covers the major decisions of October Term 2008, which ended on June 29, 2009.

As with past supplements, the new cases are presented in the context of the section of the casebook where they would fit. Brief introductory notes provide students information on how the new cases relate to the prior decisions.

Five major cases are presented. *Northwest Austin Municipal District Number One v. Holder*, involves whether it was constitutional for Congress to extend Section 5 of the Voting Rights Act for 25 years. This is presented in Chapter 2 concerning the scope of the federal legislative power.

Wyeth v. Levine is an important case concerning the scope of federal preemption and is presented in Chapter 4, under the section concerning implied preemption.

Two cases involve issues of due process. *Caperton v. A.T. Massey Coal* concerned whether due process is violated when a judge received very large contributions and expenditures from a litigant. *District Attorney's Office for the Third Judicial District v. Osborne* concerned whether due process requires access to DNA testing for a convicted criminal. These cases are presented in Chapter 8 under procedural due process.

Finally, the Court decided one major First Amendment case concerning speech, *Pleasant Grove v. Summum*, which involves whether the government may engage in content-based discrimination when it adopts private speech as its own message. This is presented in Chapter 9.

I will prepare annual supplements and look forward to the Fourth Edition in 2013. Suggestions from professors and students are invaluable and very much appreciated.

Erwin Chemerinsky
July, 2009

Chapter 2

The Federal Legislative Power

D. Congress's Powers Under the Post-Civil War Amendments

2. What Is the Scope of Congress's Power? (casebook, p. 253)

Section 5 of the Voting Rights Act of 1965 requires that jurisdictions with a history of race discrimination in voting obtain "preclearance" from the Attorney General or a federal court before changes in their election practices. This was adopted pursuant to Section 2 of the Fifteenth Amendment, which authorizes Congress to enact laws to enforce the provisions of that Amendment, which prohibits denial of the right to vote on account of race or previous condition of servitude.

In 2006, Congress extended Section 5 of the Voting Rights Act for another 25 years. In *Northwest Austin Municipal Utility District Number One v. Holder*, the Court considered, but did not decide, whether it was constitutional for Congress to extend this law. The Court avoided the constitutional issue by allowing local districts to seek to "bail out" of the law and thus avoid its requirements. If jurisdictions are denied such bail-outs, it is likely they will reassert that the statute is unconstitutional and the issue of the law's constitutionality will return to the Supreme Court.

NORTHWEST AUSTIN MUNICIPAL UTILITY DISTRICT NUMBER ONE v. HOLDER
129 S.Ct. _____ (2009)

Chief Justice ROBERTS delivered the opinion of the Court.

The plaintiff in this case is a small utility district raising a big question-the constitutionality of § 5 of the Voting Rights Act. The district has an elected board, and is required by § 5 to seek preclearance from federal authorities in Washington, D.C., before it can change anything about those elections. This is required even though there has never been any evidence of racial discrimination in voting in the district.

The district filed suit seeking relief from these preclearance obligations under the "bailout" provision of the Voting Rights Act. That provision allows the release of a "political subdivision" from the preclearance requirements if certain rigorous conditions are met. The court below denied relief, concluding that bailout was unavailable to a political subdivision like the utility district that did not register its own voters. The district appealed, arguing that the Act imposes no such limitation on bailout, and that if it does, the preclearance requirements are unconstitutional.

That constitutional question has attracted ardent briefs from dozens of interested parties, but the importance of the question does not justify our rushing to decide it. Quite the contrary: Our usual practice is to avoid the unnecessary resolution of constitutional questions. We agree that the district is eligible under the Act to seek bailout. We therefore reverse, and do not reach the constitutionality of § 5.

I

A

The Fifteenth Amendment promises that the "right of citizens of the United States to vote shall not be denied or abridged . . . on account of race, color, or previous condition of servitude." In addition to that self-executing right, the Amendment also gives Congress the "power to enforce this article by appropriate legislation." The first century of congressional enforcement of the Amendment, however, can only be regarded as a failure. Early enforcement Acts were inconsistently applied and repealed with the rise of Jim Crow. Another series of enforcement statutes in the 1950s and 1960s depended on individual lawsuits filed by the Department of Justice. But litigation is slow and expensive, and the States were creative in "contriving new rules" to continue violating the Fifteenth Amendment "in the face of adverse federal court decrees."

Congress responded with the Voting Rights Act. Section 2 of the Act operates nationwide; as it exists today, that provision forbids any "standard, practice, or procedure" that "results in a denial or abridgment of the right of any citizen of the United States to vote on account of race or color." Section 2 is not at issue in this case.

The remainder of the Act constitutes a "scheme of stringent remedies aimed at areas where voting discrimination has been most flagrant." Rather than continuing to depend on case-by-case litigation, the Act directly pre-empted the most powerful tools of black disenfranchisement in the covered areas. All literacy tests and similar voting qualifications were abolished by § 4 of the Act. Although such tests may have been facially neutral, they were easily manipulated to keep blacks from voting. The Act also empowered federal examiners to override state determinations about who was eligible to vote.

These two remedies were bolstered by § 5, which suspended all changes in state election procedure until they were submitted to and approved by a three-judge Federal District Court in Washington, D.C., or the Attorney General. Such preclearance is granted only if the change neither "has the purpose nor will have the effect of denying or abridging the right to vote on account of race or color." We have interpreted the requirements of § 5 to apply not only to the ballot-access rights guaranteed by § 4, but to drawing district lines as well.

To confine these remedies to areas of flagrant disenfranchisement, the Act applied them only to States that had used a forbidden test or device in November 1964, and had less than 50% voter registration or turnout in the 1964 Presidential election. Congress recognized that the coverage formula it had adopted "might bring within its sweep governmental units not guilty of any unlawful discriminatory voting practices." It therefore "afforded such jurisdictions immediately available protection in the form of . . . [a] 'bailout' suit."

To bail out under the current provision, a jurisdiction must seek a declaratory judgment from a three-judge District Court in Washington, D.C. It must show that for the previous 10 years it has not used any forbidden voting test, has not been subject to any valid objection under § 5, and has not been found liable for other voting rights violations; it must also show that it has "engaged in constructive efforts to eliminate intimidation and harassment" of voters, and similar measures. The Attorney General can consent to entry of judgment in favor of bailout if the evidence warrants it, though other interested parties are allowed to intervene in the declaratory judgment action. There are other restrictions: To bail out, a covered jurisdiction must show that every jurisdiction in its territory has complied with all of these requirements. The District Court also retains continuing jurisdiction over a successful bailout suit for 10 years, and may reinstate coverage if any violation is found.

As enacted, §§ 4 and 5 of the Voting Rights Act were temporary provisions. They were expected to be in effect for only five years. We upheld the temporary Voting Rights Act of 1965 as an appropriate exercise of congressional power in *Katzenbach v. South Carolina,* explaining that "[t]he constitutional propriety of the Voting Rights Act of 1965 must be judged with reference to the historical experience which it reflects." We concluded that the problems Congress faced when it passed the Act were so dire that "exceptional conditions [could] justify legislative measures not otherwise appropriate."

Congress reauthorized the Act in 1970 (for 5 years), 1975 (for 7 years), and 1982 (for 25 years). The coverage formula remained the same, based on the use of voting-eligibility tests and the rate of registration and turnout among all voters, but the pertinent dates for assessing these criteria moved from 1964 to include 1968 and eventually 1972. We upheld each of these reauthorizations against constitutional challenges, finding that circumstances continued to justify the provisions. Most recently, in 2006, Congress extended § 5 for yet another 25 years. The 2006 Act retained 1972 as the last baseline year for triggering coverage under § 5. It is that latest extension that is now before us.

B

Northwest Austin Municipal Utility District Number One was created in 1987 to deliver city services to residents of a portion of Travis County, Texas. It is governed by a board of five members, elected to staggered terms of four years. The district does not register voters but is responsible for its own elections; for administrative reasons, those elections are run by Travis County. Because the district is located in Texas, it is subject to the obligations of § 5, although there is no evidence that it has ever discriminated on the basis of race.

The district filed suit in the District Court for the District of Columbia, seeking relief under the statute's bailout provisions and arguing in the alternative that, if interpreted to render the district ineligible for bailout, § 5 was unconstitutional.

II

The historic accomplishments of the Voting Rights Act are undeniable. When it was first passed, unconstitutional discrimination was rampant and the "registration of voting-age whites ran roughly 50 percentage points or more ahead" of black registration in many covered States. Today, the registration gap between white and black voters is in single digits in the covered States; in some of those States, blacks now register and vote at higher rates than whites. Similar dramatic improvements have occurred for other racial minorities. "[M]any of the first generation barriers to minority voter registration and voter turnout that were in place prior to the [Voting Rights Act] have been eliminated."

At the same time, § 5, "which authorizes federal intrusion into sensitive areas of state and local policymaking, imposes substantial 'federalism costs.'" These federalism costs have caused Members of this Court to express serious misgivings about the constitutionality of § 5.

Section 5 goes beyond the prohibition of the Fifteenth Amendment by suspending *all* changes to state election law—however innocuous—until they have been precleared by federal authorities in Washington, D.C. The preclearance requirement applies broadly, and in particular to every political subdivision in a covered State, no matter how small.

Some of the conditions that we relied upon in upholding this statutory scheme have unquestionably improved. Things have changed in the South. Voter turnout and registration rates now approach parity. Blatantly discriminatory evasions of federal decrees are rare. And minority candidates hold office at unprecedented levels.

These improvements are no doubt due in significant part to the Voting Rights Act itself, and stand as a monument to its success. Past success alone, however, is not adequate justification to retain the preclearance requirements. It may be that these improvements are insufficient and that conditions continue to warrant preclearance under the Act. But the Act imposes current burdens and must be justified by current needs.

The Act also differentiates between the States, despite our historic tradition that all the States enjoy "equal sovereignty." Distinctions can be justified in some cases. "The doctrine of the equality of States . . . does not bar . . . remedies for *local* evils which have subsequently appeared." But a departure from the fundamental principle of equal sovereignty requires a showing that a statute's disparate geographic coverage is sufficiently related to the problem that it targets. These federalism concerns are underscored by the argument that the preclearance requirements in one State would be unconstitutional in another.

The evil that § 5 is meant to address may no longer be concentrated in the jurisdictions singled out for preclearance. The statute's coverage formula is based on data that is now more than 35 years old, and there is considerable evidence that it fails to account for current political conditions. For example, the racial gap in voter registration and turnout is lower in the States originally covered by § 5 than it is nationwide. Congress heard warnings from supporters of extending § 5 that the evidence in the record did not address "systematic differences between the covered and the non-covered areas of the United States[,] . . . and, in fact, the evidence that is in the record suggests that there is more similarity than difference."

The parties do not agree on the standard to apply in deciding whether, in light of the foregoing concerns, Congress exceeded its Fifteenth Amendment enforcement power in extending the preclearance requirements. The district argues that "[t]here must be a congruence and proportionality between the injury to be prevented or remedied and the means adopted to that end"; the Federal Government asserts that it is enough that the legislation be a "rational means to effectuate the constitutional prohibition." That question has been extensively briefed in this case, but we need not resolve it. The Act's preclearance requirements and its coverage formula raise serious constitutional questions under either test.

In assessing those questions, we are keenly mindful of our institutional role. We fully appreciate that judging the constitutionality of an Act of Congress is "the gravest and most delicate duty that this Court is called on to perform." "The Congress is a coequal branch of government whose Members take the same oath we do to uphold the Constitution of the United States." The Fifteenth Amendment empowers "Congress," not the Court, to determine in the first instance what legislation is needed to enforce it. Congress amassed a sizable record in support of its decision to extend the preclearance requirements, a record the District Court determined "document[ed] contemporary racial discrimination in covered states." The District Court also found that the record "demonstrat[ed] that section 5 prevents discriminatory voting changes" by "quietly but effectively deterring discriminatory changes."

We will not shrink from our duty "as the bulwar[k] of a limited constitution against legislative encroachments," The Federalist No. 78, p. 526 (J. Cooke ed. 1961) (A. Hamilton), but "[i]t is a well-established principle governing the prudent exercise of this Court's jurisdiction that normally the Court will not decide a constitutional question if there is some other ground upon which to dispose of the case." Here, the district also raises a statutory claim that it is eligible to bail out under §§ 4 and 5.

Justice Thomas argues that the principle of constitutional avoidance has no pertinence here. He contends that even if we resolve the district's statutory argument in its favor, we would still have to reach the constitutional question, because the district's statutory argument would not afford it all the relief it seeks.

We disagree. The district expressly describes its constitutional challenge to § 5 as being "in the alternative" to its statutory argument. We therefore turn to the district's statutory argument.

III

Section 4(b) of the Voting Rights Act authorizes a bailout suit by a "State or political subdivision." There is no dispute that the district is a political subdivision of the State of Texas in the ordinary sense of the term. The district was created under Texas law with "powers of government" relating to local utilities and natural resources.

The Act, however, also provides a narrower statutory definition in § 14(c)(2): " '[P]olitical subdivision' shall mean any county or parish, except that where registration for voting is not conducted under the supervision of a county or parish, the term shall include any other subdivision of a State which conducts registration for voting." The District Court concluded that this definition applied to the bailout provision in § 4(a), and that the district did not qualify, since it is not a county or parish and does not conduct its own voter registration.

Were the scope of § 4(a) considered in isolation from the rest of the statute and our prior cases, the District Court's approach might well be correct. But here specific precedent, the structure of the Voting Rights Act, and underlying constitutional concerns compel a broader reading of the bailout provision. We hold that all political subdivisions—not only those described in § 14(c)(2)—are eligible to file a bailout suit.

More than 40 years ago, this Court concluded that "exceptional conditions" prevailing in certain parts of the country justified extraordinary legislation otherwise unfamiliar to our federal system. In part due to the success of that legislation, we are now a very different Nation. Whether conditions continue to justify such legislation is a difficult constitutional question we do not answer today. We conclude instead that the Voting Rights Act permits all political subdivisions, including the district in this case, to seek relief from its preclearance requirements.

Justice THOMAS, concurring in the judgment in part and dissenting in part.

This appeal presents two questions: first, whether appellant is entitled to bail out from coverage under the Voting Rights Act of 1965 (VRA); and second, whether the preclearance requirement of § 5 of the VRA is unconstitutional. Because the Court's statutory decision does not provide appellant with full relief, I conclude that it is inappropriate to apply the constitutional avoidance doctrine in this case. I would therefore decide the constitutional issue presented and hold that § 5 exceeds Congress' power to enforce the Fifteenth Amendment.

I

The doctrine of constitutional avoidance factors heavily in the Court's conclusion that appellant is eligible for bailout as a "political subdivision" under § 4(a) of the VRA. Regardless of the Court's resolution of the statutory question, I am in full agreement that this case raises serious questions concerning the constitutionality of § 5 of the VRA. But, unlike the Court, I do not believe that the doctrine of constitutional avoidance is applicable here. The ultimate relief sought in this case is not bailout eligibility—it is bailout itself.

Eligibility for bailout turns on the statutory question addressed by the Court—the proper definition of "political subdivision" in the bailout clauses of § 4(a) of the VRA. Entitlement to bailout, however, requires a covered "political subdivision" to submit substantial evidence indicating that it is not engaging in "discrimination in voting on account of race." The Court properly declines to give appellant bailout because appellant has not yet proved its compliance with the statutory requirements for such relief. In fact, the record below shows that appellant's factual entitlement to bailout is a vigorously contested issue. Given its resolution of the statutory question, the Court has thus correctly remanded the case for resolution of appellant's factual entitlement to bailout.

But because the Court is not in a position to award appellant bailout, adjudication of the constitutionality of § 5, in my view, cannot be avoided. "Traditionally, the avoidance canon was not a doctrine under which courts read statutes to avoid mere constitutional doubts. Instead, it commanded courts, when faced with two plausible constructions of a statute—one constitutional and the other unconstitutional—to choose the constitutional reading." To the extent that constitutional avoidance is a worthwhile tool of statutory construction, it is because it allows a court to dispose of an entire case on grounds that do not require the court to pass on a statute's constitutionality. Absent a determination that appellant is not just eligible for bailout, but is entitled to it, this case will not have been entirely disposed of on a nonconstitutional ground. Invocation of the doctrine of constitutional avoidance is therefore inappropriate in this case.

The doctrine of constitutional avoidance is also unavailable here because an interpretation of § 4(a) that merely makes more political subdivisions *eligible* for bailout does not render § 5 constitutional and the Court notably does not suggest otherwise. Bailout eligibility is a distant prospect for most covered jurisdictions.

II

The Court quite properly alerts Congress that § 5 tests the outer boundaries of its Fifteenth Amendment enforcement authority and may not be constitutional. And, although I respect the Court's careful approach to this weighty issue, I nevertheless believe it is necessary to definitively resolve that important question. For the reasons set forth below, I conclude that the lack of current evidence of intentional discrimination with respect to voting renders § 5 unconstitutional. The provision can no longer be justified as an appropriate mechanism for enforcement of the Fifteenth Amendment.

The extensive pattern of discrimination that led the Court to previously uphold § 5 as enforcing the Fifteenth Amendment no longer exists. Covered jurisdictions are not now engaged in a systematic campaign to deny black citizens access to the ballot through intimidation and violence. And the days of "grandfather clauses, property qualifications, 'good character' tests, and the requirement that registrants 'understand' or 'interpret' certain matter," are gone. There is thus currently no concerted effort in these jurisdictions to engage in the "unremitting and ingenious defiance of the Constitution," that served as the constitutional basis for upholding the "uncommon exercise of congressional power" embodied in § 5.

The lack of sufficient evidence that the covered jurisdictions currently engage in the type of discrimination that underlay the enactment of § 5 undermines any basis for retaining it. Punishment for long past sins is not a legitimate basis for imposing a forward-looking preventative measure that has already served its purpose. Those supporting § 5's reenactment argue that without it these jurisdictions would return to the racially discriminatory practices of 30 and 40 years ago. But there is no evidence that public officials stand ready, if given the chance, to again engage in concerted acts of violence, terror, and subterfuge in order to keep minorities from voting. Without such evidence, the charge can only be premised on outdated assumptions about racial attitudes in the covered jurisdictions. Admitting that a prophylactic law as broad as § 5 is no longer constitutionally justified based on current evidence of discrimination is not a sign of defeat. It is an acknowledgment of victory.

The current statistical evidence confirms that the emergency that prompted the enactment of § 5 has long since passed. By 2006, the voter registration rates for blacks in Alabama, Louisiana, and Mississippi had jumped to 71.8%, 66.9%, and 72.2%, respectively. Therefore, in contrast to the *Katzenbach* Court's finding that the "registration of voting-age whites ran roughly 50 percentage points or more ahead of Negro registration" in these States in 1964, since that time this disparity has nearly vanished. In 2006, the disparity was only 3 percentage points in Alabama, 8 percentage points in Louisiana, and in Mississippi, black voter registration actually exceeded white voter registration by 1.5 percentage points. In addition, blacks in these three covered States also have higher registration numbers than the registration rate for whites in noncovered states.

Indeed, when reenacting § 5 in 2006, Congress evidently understood that the emergency conditions which prompted § 5's original enactment no longer exist. Instead of relying on the kind of evidence that the *Katzenbach* Court had found so persuasive, Congress instead based reenactment on evidence of what it termed "second generation barriers constructed to prevent minority voters from fully participating in the electoral process." But such evidence is not probative of the type of purposeful discrimination that prompted Congress to enact § 5 in 1965. For example, Congress relied upon evidence of racially polarized voting within the covered jurisdictions. But racially polarized voting is not evidence of unconstitutional discrimination, is not state action, and is not a problem unique to the South.

This is not to say that voter discrimination is extinct. Indeed, the District Court singled out a handful of examples of allegedly discriminatory voting practices from the record made by Congress. But the existence of discrete and isolated incidents of interference with the right to vote has never been sufficient justification for the imposition of § 5's extraordinary requirements. From its inception, the statute was promoted as a measure needed to neutralize a coordinated and unrelenting campaign to deny an entire race access to the ballot. Perfect compliance with the Fifteenth Amendment's substantive command is not now—nor has it ever been—the yardstick for determining whether Congress has the power to employ broad prophylactic legislation to enforce that Amendment. The burden remains with Congress to prove that the extreme circumstances warranting § 5's enactment persist today. A record of scattered infringement of the right to vote is not a constitutionally acceptable substitute.

In 1870, the Fifteenth Amendment was ratified in order to guarantee that no citizen would be denied the right to vote based on race, color, or previous condition of servitude. Congress passed § 5 of the VRA in 1965 because that promise had remained unfulfilled for far too long. But now—more than 40 years later—the violence, intimidation, and subterfuge that led Congress to pass § 5 and this Court to uphold it no longer remains. An acknowledgment of § 5's unconstitutionality represents a fulfillment of the Fifteenth Amendment's promise of full enfranchisement and honors the success achieved by the VRA.

Chapter 4

Limits on State Regulatory and Taxing Power

A. Preemption of State and Local Laws

1. Express Preemption (casebook, p. 436)

In *Altria v. Good,* as in *Lorillard Tobacco Co. v. Riley*, the Supreme Court considered the meaning of an express preemption provision in a federal law regulating labeling of cigarettes. The issue in *Altria* was whether the federal law barred state tort liability for fraud in marketing low tar and nicotine cigarettes.

ALTRIA GROUP, INC. v. GOOD
129 S.Ct. 558 (2008)

JUSTICE STEVENS delivered the opinion of the Court.

Respondents, who have for over 15 years smoked "light" cigarettes manufactured by petitioners, Philip Morris USA, Inc., and its parent company, Altria Group, Inc., claim that petitioners violated the Maine Unfair Trade Practices Act (MUTPA). Specifically, they allege that petitioners' advertising fraudulently conveyed the message that their "light" cigarettes deliver less tar and nicotine to consumers than regular brands despite petitioners' knowledge that the message was untrue. Petitioners deny the charge, asserting that their advertisements were factually accurate. The merits of the dispute are not before us because the District Court entered summary judgment in favor of petitioners on the ground that respondents' state-law claim is pre-empted by the Federal Cigarette Labeling and Advertising Act, as amended (Labeling Act). The Court of Appeals reversed that judgment, and we granted certiorari to review its holding that the Labeling Act neither expressly nor impliedly pre-empts respondents' fraud claim. We affirm.

I

Respondents are Maine residents and longtime smokers of Marlboro Lights and Cambridge Lights cigarettes, which are manufactured by petitioners. Invoking the diversity jurisdiction of the Federal District Court, respondents filed a complaint alleging that petitioners deliberately deceived them about the true and harmful nature of "light" cigarettes in violation of the MUTPA. Respondents claim that petitioners fraudulently marketed their cigarettes as being "light" and containing "[l]owered [t]ar and [n]icotine" to convey to consumers that they deliver less tar and nicotine and are therefore less harmful than regular cigarettes.

II

Article VI, cl. 2, of the Constitution provides that the laws of the United States "shall be the supreme Law of the Land; . . . any Thing in the Constitution or Laws of any state to the Contrary notwithstanding." Consistent with that command, we have long recognized that state laws that conflict with federal law are "without effect."

Our inquiry into the scope of a statute's pre-emptive effect is guided by the rule that "[t]he purpose of Congress is the ultimate touchstone in every pre-emption case." Congress may indicate pre-emptive intent through a statute's express language or through its structure and purpose. If a federal law contains an express pre-emption clause, it does not immediately end the inquiry because the question of the substance and scope of Congress' displacement of state law still remains. Pre-emptive intent may also be inferred if the scope of the statute indicates that Congress intended federal law to occupy the legislative field, or if there is an actual conflict between state and federal law.

When addressing questions of express or implied pre-emption, we begin our analysis "with the assumption that the historic police powers of the States [are] not to be superseded by the Federal Act unless that was the clear and manifest purpose of Congress." That assumption applies with particular force when Congress has legislated in a field traditionally occupied by the States. Thus, when the text of a pre-emption clause is susceptible of more than one plausible reading, courts ordinarily "accept the reading that disfavors pre-emption."

Congress enacted the Labeling Act in 1965 in response to the Surgeon General's determination that cigarette smoking is harmful to health. The

Act required that every package of cigarettes sold in the United States contain a conspicuous warning, and it pre-empted state-law positive enactments that added to the federally prescribed warning. Congress amended the Labeling Act a few years later by enacting the Public Health Cigarette Smoking Act of 1969. The amendments strengthened the language of the prescribed warning, and prohibited cigarette advertising in "any medium of electronic communication subject to [FCC] jurisdiction." They also broadened the Labeling Act's pre-emption provision. The Labeling Act has since been amended further to require cigarette manufacturers to include four more explicit warnings in their packaging and advertisements on a rotating basis.

The stated purpose of the Labeling Act is "to establish a comprehensive Federal program to deal with cigarette labeling and advertising with respect to any relationship between smoking and health, whereby—

(1) the public may be adequately informed that cigarette smoking may be hazardous to health by inclusion of a warning to that effect on each package of cigarettes; and

(2) commerce and the national economy may be (A) protected to the maximum extent consistent with this declared policy and (B) not impeded by diverse, nonuniform, and confusing cigarette labeling and advertising regulations with respect to any relationship between smoking and health.

As amended, the Labeling Act contains two express pre-emption provisions. Section 5(a) protects cigarette manufacturers from inconsistent state labeling laws by prohibiting the requirement of additional statements relating to smoking and health on cigarette packages. Section 5(b), which is at issue in this case, provides that "[n]o requirement or prohibition based on smoking and health shall be imposed under State law with respect to the advertising or promotion of any cigarettes the packages of which are labeled in conformity with the provisions of this chapter."

Together, the labeling requirement and pre-emption provisions express Congress' determination that the prescribed federal warnings are both necessary and sufficient to achieve its purpose of informing the public of the health consequences of smoking. Because Congress has decided that no additional warning statement is needed to attain that goal, States may not impede commerce in cigarettes by enforcing rules that are based on an assumption that the federal warnings are inadequate. Although both of the Act's purposes are furthered by prohibiting States from supplementing the federally prescribed warning, neither would be served by limiting the States' authority to prohibit deceptive statements in cigarette advertising.

Although it is clear that fidelity to the Act's purposes does not demand the pre-emption of state fraud rules, the principal question that we must decide is whether the text of § 1334(b) nevertheless requires that result.

III

Respondents' claim that the deceptive statements "light" and "lowered tar and nicotine" induced them to purchase petitioners' product alleges a breach of the duty not to deceive. To be sure, the presence of the federally mandated warnings may bear on the materiality of petitioners' allegedly fraudulent statements, "but that possibility does not change [respondents'] case from one about the statements into one about the warnings."

It is true, as petitioners argue, that the appeal of their advertising is based on the relationship between smoking and health. And although respondents have expressly repudiated any claim for damages for personal injuries, their actual injuries likely encompass harms to health as well as the monetary injuries they allege. These arguments are unavailing, however, because the text of § 1334(b) does not refer to *harms* related to smoking and health. Rather, it pre-empts only *requirements and prohibitions i.e.,* rules—that are based on smoking and health. The MUTPA says nothing about either "smoking" or "health." It is a general rule that creates a duty not to deceive.

In sum, we conclude now, as the plurality did in *Cipollone,* that "the phrase 'based on smoking and health' fairly but narrowly construed does not encompass the more general duty not to make fraudulent statements."

IV

As an alternative to their express pre-emption argument, petitioners contend that respondents' claim is impliedly pre-empted because, if allowed to proceed, it would present an obstacle to a longstanding policy of the FTC. According to petitioners, the FTC has for decades promoted the development and consumption of low tar cigarettes and has encouraged consumers to rely on representations of tar and nicotine content based on Cambridge Filter Method testing in choosing among cigarette brands. Even if such a regulatory policy could provide a basis for obstacle pre-emption, petitioners' description of the FTC's actions in this regard are inaccurate. The Government itself disavows any policy authorizing the use of "light" and "low tar" descriptors.

In 1966, following the publication of the Surgeon General's report on smoking and health, the FTC issued an industry guidance stating its view that "a factual statement of the tar and nicotine content (expressed in milligrams) of the mainstream smoke from a cigarette," as measured by Cambridge Filter Method testing, would not violate the FTC Act. The Commission made clear, however, that the guidance applied only to factual assertions of tar and nicotine yields and did not invite "collateral representations . . . made, expressly or by implication, as to reduction or elimination of health hazards." A year later, the FTC reiterated its position in a letter to the National Association of Broadcasters. The letter explained that, as a "general rule," the Commission would not challenge statements of tar and nicotine content when "they are shown to be accurate and fully substantiated by tests conducted in accordance with the [Cambridge Filter Method]." In 1970, the FTC considered providing further guidance, proposing a rule that would have required manufacturers to disclose tar and nicotine yields as measured by Cambridge Filter Method testing. The leading cigarette manufacturers responded by submitting a voluntary agreement under which they would disclose tar and nicotine content in their advertising, and the FTC suspended its rulemaking.

Based on these events, petitioners assert that "the FTC has *required* tobacco companies to disclose tar and nicotine yields in cigarette advertising using a government-mandated testing methodology and has *authorized* them to use descriptors as shorthand references to those numerical test results." As the foregoing history shows, however, the FTC has in fact never required that cigarette manufacturers disclose tar and nicotine yields, nor has it condoned representations of those yields through the use of "light" or "low tar" descriptors.

Subsequent Commission actions further undermine petitioners' claim. After the tobacco companies agreed to report tar and nicotine yields as measured by the Cambridge Filter Method, the FTC continued to police cigarette companies' misleading use of test results. In 1983, the FTC responded to findings that tar and nicotine yields for Barclay cigarettes obtained through Cambridge Filter Method testing were deceptive because the cigarettes in fact delivered disproportionately more tar to smokers than other cigarettes with similar Cambridge Filter Method ratings. And in 1995, the FTC found that a manufacturer's representation "that consumers will get less tar by smoking ten packs of Carlton brand cigarettes than by smoking a single pack of the other brands" was deceptive even though it was based on the results of Cambridge Filter Method testing.

This history shows that, contrary to petitioners' suggestion, the FTC has no longstanding policy authorizing collateral representations based on Cambridge Filter Method test results. Rather, the FTC has endeavored to inform consumers of the comparative tar and nicotine content of different cigarette brands and has in some instances prevented misleading representations of Cambridge Filter Method test results. The FTC's failure to require petitioners to correct their allegedly misleading use of "light" descriptors is not evidence to the contrary; agency nonenforcement of a federal statute is not the same as a policy of approval.

V

We conclude that the Labeling Act does not pre-empt state-law claims like respondents' that are predicated on the duty not to deceive. We also hold that the FTC's various decisions with respect to statements of tar and nicotine content do not impliedly pre-empt respondents' claim. Respondents still must prove that petitioners' use of "light" and "lowered tar" descriptors in fact violated the state deceptive practices statute, but neither the Labeling Act's pre-emption provision nor the FTC's actions in this field prevent a jury from considering that claim.

JUSTICE THOMAS, with whom THE CHIEF JUSTICE, JUSTICE SCALIA, and JUSTICE ALITO join, dissenting.

[T]he question before us is whether state-law claims alleging that cigarette manufacturers misled the public about the health effects of cigarettes are pre-empted by the Federal Cigarette Labeling and Advertising Act. The Labeling Act requires that specific health warnings be placed on all cigarette packaging and advertising, in order to eliminate "diverse, nonuniform, and confusing cigarette labeling and advertising regulations with respect to any relationship between smoking and health." To that end, § 5(b) of the Labeling Act pre-empts any "requirement or prohibition based on smoking and health . . . imposed under State law with respect to the advertising or promotion of any cigarettes."

Respondents' lawsuit under the Maine Unfair Trade Practices Act (MUTPA), is expressly pre-empted under § 5(b) of the Labeling Act. The civil action is premised on the allegation that the cigarette manufacturers misled respondents into believing that smoking light cigarettes would be healthier for them than smoking regular cigarettes. A judgment in respondents' favor will thus result in a "requirement" that petitioners represent the effects of smoking on health in a particular way in their advertising and promotion of light cigarettes. Because liability in this case is thereby premised on the effect of smoking on health, I would hold that respondents' state-law claims are expressly pre-empted by § 5(b) of the Labeling Act. I respectfully dissent.

[I]

Sixteen years later, we must resolve whether respondents' class-action claims for fraudulent marketing under the MUTPA are pre-empted by § 5 (b) of the Labeling Act.

[T]here is no authority for invoking the presumption against pre-emption in express pre-emption cases. The text of the statute must control.

[E]very products liability action, including a failure-to-warn action, applies generally to *all* products. Thus, the "duty" or "rule" involved in a failure-to-warn claim is no more specific to smoking and health than is a common-law fraud claim based on the "duty" or "rule" not to use deceptive or misleading trade practices.

Furthermore, contrary to the majority's policy arguments, faithful application of the statutory language does not authorize fraudulent advertising with respect to smoking and health. Any misleading promotional statements for cigarettes remain subject to federal regulatory oversight under the Labeling Act. The relevant question thus is not whether "petitioners will be prohibited from selling as 'light' or 'low tar' only those cigarettes that are not actually light and do not actually deliver less tar and nicotine." Rather, the issue is whether the Labeling Act allows regulators and juries to decide, on a state-by-state basis, whether petitioners' light and low-tar descriptors were in fact fraudulent, or instead whether § 5(b) charged the Federal Government with reaching a comprehensive judgment with respect to this question.

Congress chose a uniform federal standard. Under the Labeling Act, Congress "establish[ed] a comprehensive Federal Program to deal with cigarette labeling and advertising," so that "commerce and the national economy may ... not [be] impeded by diverse, nonuniform, and confusing cigarette labeling and advertising regulations with respect to any relationship between smoking and health." The majority's distorted interpretation of § 5(b) defeats this express congressional purpose, opening the door to an untold number of deceptive-practices lawsuits across the country. The question whether marketing a light cigarette is "'misrepresentative'" in light of compensatory behavior "would almost certainly be answered differently from State to State." This will inevitably result in the nonuniform imposition of liability for the marketing of light and/or low-tar cigarettes—the precise problem that Congress intended § 5(b) to remedy.

[II]

Applying the proper test— *i.e.,* whether a jury verdict on respondents' claims would "impos[e] an obligation" on the cigarette manufacturer "because of the effect of smoking upon health," respondents' state-law claims are expressly pre-empted by § 5(b) of the Labeling Act. Respondents, longtime smokers of Marlboro Lights, claim that they have suffered an injury as a result of petitioners' decision to advertise these cigarettes as "light" and/or "low-tar and low nicotine products." They claim that petitioners marketed their cigarettes as "light" and/or "low-tar and low-nicotine products" despite knowledge that light-cigarette smokers would engage in compensatory behavior causing them to inhale at least as much tar and nicotine as smokers of regular cigarettes. Respondents thus allege that they were misled into thinking that they were gaining a health advantage by smoking the light cigarettes, and, as a result, petitioners' conduct was an "unfair or deceptive act or practice" under the MUTPA.

Respondents' claims seek to impose liability on petitioners because of the effect that smoking light cigarettes had on their health. The alleged misrepresentation here—that "light" and "low-tar" cigarettes are not as healthy as advertised—is actionable *only* because of the effect that smoking light and low-tar cigarettes had on respondents' health. Otherwise, any alleged misrepresentation about the effect of the cigarettes on health would be immaterial for purposes of the MUTPA and would not be the source of the injuries that provided the impetus for the class-action lawsuit. Therefore, with this suit, respondents seek to *require* the cigarette manufacturers to provide additional warnings about compensatory behavior, or to *prohibit* them from selling these products with the "light" or "low-tar" descriptors. This is exactly the type of lawsuit that is pre-empted by the Labeling Act.

Because the proper test for pre-emption is to look at the factual basis of a complaint to determine if a claim imposes a requirement based on smoking and health, there is no meaningful distinction to be drawn in this case between common-law failure-to-warn claims and claims under the MUTPA. As the majority readily admits, both types of claims impose duties with respect to the same conduct— *i.e.,* the marketing of "light," "low-tar," and "low-nicotine" cigarettes. If the claims arise from identical conduct, the claims impose the same requirement or prohibition with respect to that conduct. And when that allegedly wrongful conduct involves misleading statements about the health effects of smoking a particular brand of cigarette, the liability and resulting requirement or prohibition are, by definition, based on smoking and health.

Because I believe that respondents' claims are pre-empted under § 5 (b) of the Labeling Act, I respectfully dissent.

———

When Congress has the authority to legislate, it can exclude within a statute a provision expressly preempting state regulation in the area. In *Altria Group, Inc. v. Good*, 129 S.Ct. 538 (2008), the Court considered the scope of the preemption provision in the federal Cigarette Label and Advertising Act. The provision at issue, Section 5(b), provides that "[n]o requirement or prohibition based on smoking and health shall be imposed under State law with respect to the advertising or promotion of any cigarettes the packages of which are labeled in conformity with the provisions of this chapter."

The question before the Court was whether this provision preempted suit against cigarette companies, under the Maine Unfair Trade Practices Act, for fraud in marketing and advertising low tar and nicotine cigarettes. In a 5-4 decision, with Justice Stevens writing for the majority, the Court concluded that there was not preemption. Justice Stevens stressed "[w]hen the text of an express pre-emption clause is susceptible of more than one plausible reading, courts ordinarily accept the reading that disfavors pre-emption." The Court concluded that "the phrase 'based on smoking and health' fairly but narrowly construed does not encompass the more general duty not to make fraudulent statements." Thus, tobacco companies could be sued for fraud in the marketing of "light" cigarettes.

2. Implied Preemption

a. *Conflicts Preemption (casebook, p. 443)*

If federal law and state law conflict, such as if they are mutually exclusive, then the state law is preempted. But this inevitably raises the question of whether the federal law is the minimum of regulation and states can go further, or if it is the maximum of regulation and states cannot add to it. This is the question in *Wyeth v. Levine*, which raised the issue of whether approval of a prescription drug warning label precluded state tort liability on a failure-to-warn theory.

WYETH v. LEVINE
129 S.Ct. 1187 (2009)

Justice STEVENS delivered the opinion of the Court.

Directly injecting the drug Phenergan into a patient's vein creates a significant risk of catastrophic consequences. A Vermont jury found that petitioner Wyeth, the manufacturer of the drug, had failed to provide an adequate warning of that risk and awarded damages to respondent Diana Levine to compensate her for the amputation of her arm. The warnings on Phenergan's label had been deemed sufficient by the federal Food and Drug Administration (FDA) when it approved Wyeth's new drug application in 1955 and when it later approved changes in the drug's labeling. The question we must decide is whether the FDA's approvals provide Wyeth with a complete defense to Levine's tort claims. We conclude that they do not.

I

Phenergan is Wyeth's brand name for promethazine hydrochloride, an antihistamine used to treat nausea. The injectable form of Phenergan can be administered intramuscularly or intravenously, and it can be administered intravenously through either the "IV-push" method, whereby the drug is injected directly into a patient's vein, or the "IV-drip" method, whereby the drug is introduced into a saline solution in a hanging intravenous bag and slowly descends through a catheter inserted in a patient's vein. The drug is corrosive and causes irreversible gangrene if it enters a patient's artery.

Levine's injury resulted from an IV-push injection of Phenergan. On April 7, 2000, as on previous visits to her local clinic for treatment of a migraine headache, she received an intramuscular injection of Demerol for her headache and Phenergan for her nausea. Because the combination did not provide relief, she returned later that day and received a second injection of both drugs. This time, the physician assistant administered the drugs by the IV-push method, and Phenergan entered Levine's artery, either because the needle penetrated an artery directly or because the drug escaped from the vein into surrounding tissue (a phenomenon called "perivascular extravasation") where it came in contact with arterial blood. As a result, Levine developed gangrene, and doctors amputated first her right hand and then her entire forearm. In addition to her pain and suffering, Levine incurred substantial medical expenses and the loss of her livelihood as a professional musician.

After settling claims against the health center and clinician, Levine brought an action for damages against Wyeth, relying on common-law negligence and strict-liability theories. Although Phenergan's labeling warned of the danger of gangrene and amputation following inadvertent intra-arterial injection, Levine alleged that the labeling was defective because it failed to instruct clinicians to use the IV-drip method of intravenous administration instead of the higher risk IV-push method. More broadly, she alleged that Phenergan is not reasonably safe for intravenous administration because the foreseeable risks of gangrene and loss of limb are great in relation to the drug's therapeutic benefits.

Wyeth filed a motion for summary judgment, arguing that Levine's failure-to-warn claims were pre-empted by federal law. The court found no merit in Wyeth's pre-emption argument. Answering questions on a special verdict form, the jury found that Wyeth was negligent, that Phenergan was a defective product as a result of inadequate warnings and instructions, and that no intervening cause had broken the causal connection between the product defects and the plaintiff's injury. It awarded total damages of $7,400,000, which the court reduced to account for Levine's earlier settlement with the health center and clinician. The Vermont Supreme Court affirmed.

II

Wyeth makes two separate pre-emption arguments: first, that it would have been impossible for it to comply with the state-law duty to modify Phenergan's labeling without violating federal law, and second, that recognition of Levine's state tort action creates an unacceptable "obstacle to the accomplishment and execution of the full purposes and objectives of Congress," because it substitutes a lay jury's decision about drug labeling for the expert judgment of the FDA. As a preface to our evaluation of these arguments, we identify two factual propositions decided during the trial court proceedings, emphasize two legal principles that guide our analysis, and review the history of the controlling federal statute.

The trial court proceedings established that Levine's injury would not have occurred if Phenergan's label had included an adequate warning about the risks of the IV-push method of administering the drug. The record contains evidence that the physician assistant administered a greater dose than the label prescribed, that she may have inadvertently injected the drug into an artery rather than a vein, and that she continued to inject the drug after Levine complained of pain. Nevertheless, the jury rejected Wyeth's argument that the clinician's conduct was an intervening cause that absolved it of liability. In finding Wyeth negligent as well as strictly liable, the jury also determined that Levine's injury was foreseeable. That the inadequate label was both a but-for and proximate cause of Levine's injury is supported by the record and no longer challenged by Wyeth.

The trial court proceedings further established that the critical defect in Phenergan's label was the lack of an adequate warning about the risks of IV-push administration. But, as the Vermont Supreme Court explained, the jury verdict established only that Phenergan's warning was insufficient. It did not mandate a particular replacement warning, nor did it require contraindicating IV-push administration: We therefore need not decide whether a state rule proscribing intravenous administration would be pre-empted. The narrower question presented is whether federal law pre-empts Levine's claim that Phenergan's label did not contain an adequate warning about using the IV-push method of administration.

Our answer to that question must be guided by two cornerstones of our pre-emption jurisprudence. First, "the purpose of Congress is the ultimate touchstone in every pre-emption case." Second, "[i]n all pre-emption cases, and particularly in those in which Congress has 'legislated . . . in a field which the States have traditionally occupied,' . . . we 'start with the assumption that the historic police powers of the States were not to be superseded by the Federal Act unless that was the clear and manifest purpose of Congress.'"

III

Wyeth first argues that Levine's state-law claims are pre-empted because it is impossible for it to comply with both the state-law duties underlying those claims and its federal labeling duties. The FDA's premarket approval of a new drug application includes the approval of the exact text in the proposed label. Generally speaking, a manufacturer may only change a drug label after the FDA approves a supplemental application. There is, however, an FDA regulation that permits a manufacturer to make certain changes to its label before receiving the agency's approval. Among other things, this "changes being effected" (CBE) regulation provides that if a manufacturer is changing a label to "add or strengthen a contraindication, warning, precaution, or adverse reaction" or to "add or strengthen an instruction about dosage and administration that is intended to increase the safe use of the drug product," it may make the labeling change upon filing its supplemental application with the FDA; it need not wait for FDA approval.

Wyeth argues that the CBE regulation is not implicated in this case because a 2008 amendment provides that a manufacturer may only change its label "to reflect newly acquired information." Resting on this language (which Wyeth argues simply reaffirmed the interpretation of the regulation in effect when this case was tried), Wyeth contends that it could have changed Phenergan's label only in response to new information that the FDA had not considered. And it maintains that Levine has not pointed to any such information concerning the risks of IV-push administration. Thus, Wyeth insists, it was impossible for it to discharge its state-law obligation to provide a stronger warning about IV-push administration without violating federal law. Wyeth's argument misapprehends both the federal drug regulatory scheme and its burden in establishing a pre-emption defense.

Wyeth could have revised Phenergan's label even in accordance with the amended regulation. As the FDA explained in its notice of the final rule, "newly acquired information" is not limited to new data, but also encompasses "new analyses of previously submitted data." The rule accounts for the fact that risk information accumulates over time and that the same data may take on a different meaning in light of subsequent developments.

Wyeth argues that if it had unilaterally added such a warning, it would have violated federal law governing unauthorized distribution and misbranding. Its argument that a change in Phenergan's labeling would have subjected it to liability for unauthorized distribution rests on the assumption that this labeling change would have rendered Phenergan a new drug lacking an effective application. But strengthening the warning about IV-push administration would not have made Phenergan a new drug. Nor would this warning have rendered Phenergan misbranded. The FDCA does not provide that a drug is misbranded simply because the manufacturer has altered an FDA-approved label; instead, the misbranding provision focuses on the substance of the label and, among other things, proscribes labels that fail to include "adequate warnings."

Of course, the FDA retains authority to reject labeling changes made pursuant to the CBE regulation in its review of the manufacturer's supplemental application, just as it retains such authority in reviewing all supplemental applications. But absent clear evidence that the FDA would not have approved a change to Phenergan's label, we will not conclude that it was impossible for Wyeth to comply with both federal and state requirements. Wyeth has offered no such evidence.

Impossibility pre-emption is a demanding defense. On the record before us, Wyeth has failed to demonstrate that it was impossible for it to comply with both federal and state requirements. The CBE regulation permitted Wyeth to unilaterally strengthen its warning, and the mere fact that the FDA approved Phenergan's label does not establish that it would have prohibited such a change.

IV

Wyeth also argues that requiring it to comply with a state-law duty to provide a stronger warning about IV-push administration would obstruct the purposes and objectives of federal drug labeling regulation. Levine's tort claims, it maintains, are pre-empted because they interfere with

"Congress's purpose to entrust an expert agency to make drug labeling decisions that strike a balance between competing objectives." We find no merit in this argument, which relies on an untenable interpretation of congressional intent and an overbroad view of an agency's power to pre-empt state law.

Wyeth contends that the FDCA establishes both a floor and a ceiling for drug regulation: Once the FDA has approved a drug's label, a state-law verdict may not deem the label inadequate, regardless of whether there is any evidence that the FDA has considered the stronger warning at issue. The most glaring problem with this argument is that all evidence of Congress' purposes is to the contrary. Building on its 1906 Act, Congress enacted the FDCA to bolster consumer protection against harmful products. Congress did not provide a federal remedy for consumers harmed by unsafe or ineffective drugs in the 1938 statute or in any subsequent amendment. Evidently, it determined that widely available state rights of action provided appropriate relief for injured consumers. It may also have recognized that state-law remedies further consumer protection by motivating manufacturers to produce safe and effective drugs and to give adequate warnings.

If Congress thought state-law suits posed an obstacle to its objectives, it surely would have enacted an express pre-emption provision at some point during the FDCA's 70-year history. But despite its 1976 enactment of an express pre-emption provision for medical devices, Congress has not enacted such a provision for prescription drugs. Its silence on the issue, coupled with its certain awareness of the prevalence of state tort litigation, is powerful evidence that Congress did not intend FDA oversight to be the exclusive means of ensuring drug safety and effectiveness.

In keeping with Congress' decision not to pre-empt common-law tort suits, it appears that the FDA traditionally regarded state law as a complementary form of drug regulation. The FDA has limited resources to monitor the 11,000 drugs on the market, and manufacturers have superior access to information about their drugs, especially in the post-marketing phase as new risks emerge. State tort suits uncover unknown drug hazards and provide incentives for drug manufacturers to disclose safety risks promptly. They also serve a distinct compensatory function that may motivate injured persons to come forward with information. Failure-to-warn actions, in particular, lend force to the FDCA's premise that manufacturers, not the FDA, bear primary responsibility for their drug labeling at all times. Thus, the FDA long maintained that state law offers an additional, and important, layer of consumer protection that complements FDA regulation.

V

We conclude that it is not impossible for Wyeth to comply with its state and federal law obligations and that Levine's common-law claims do not stand as an obstacle to the accomplishment of Congress' purposes in the FDCA.

Justice THOMAS, concurring in the judgment.

I agree with the Court that the fact that the Food and Drug Administration (FDA) approved the label for petitioner Wyeth's drug Phenergan does not pre-empt the state-law judgment before the Court. I write separately, however, because I cannot join the majority's implicit endorsement of far-reaching implied pre-emption doctrines. In particular, I have become increasingly skeptical of this Court's "purposes and objectives" pre-emption jurisprudence. Under this approach, the Court routinely invalidates state laws based on perceived conflicts with broad federal policy objectives, legislative history, or generalized notions of congressional purposes that are not embodied within the text of federal law. Because implied pre-emption doctrines that wander far from the statutory text are inconsistent with the Constitution, I concur only in the judgment.

In order "to ensure the protection of our fundamental liberties," the "Constitution establishes a system of dual sovereignty between the States and the Federal Government." The Framers adopted this "constitutionally mandated balance of power," to "reduce the risk of tyranny and abuse from either front," because a "federalist structure of joint sovereigns preserves to the people numerous advantages," such as "a decentralized government that will be more sensitive to the diverse needs of a heterogeneous society" and "increase[d] opportunity for citizen involvement in democratic processes." Furthermore, as the Framers observed, the "compound republic of America" provides "a double security . . . to the rights of the people" because "the power surrendered by the people is first divided between two distinct governments, and then the portion allotted to each subdivided among distinct and separate departments." The Federalist No. 51, p. 266 (M. Beloff ed., 2d ed.1987).

Under this federalist system, "the States possess sovereignty concurrent with that of the Federal Government, subject only to limitations imposed by the Supremacy Clause." In this way, the Supremacy Clause gives the Federal Government "a decided advantage in [a] delicate balance" between federal and state sovereigns. "As long as it is acting within the powers granted it under the Constitution, Congress may impose its will on the States." That is an "extraordinary power in a federalist system."

In light of these constitutional principles, I have become "increasing[ly] reluctan[t] to expand federal statutes beyond their terms through doctrines of implied pre-emption." My review of this Court's broad implied pre-emption precedents, particularly its "purposes and objectives" pre-emption jurisprudence, has increased my concerns that implied pre-emption doctrines have not always been constitutionally applied. Under the vague and "potentially boundless" doctrine of "purposes and objectives" pre-emption, in [this case], the relevant federal law did not give Wyeth a right that the state-law judgment took away, and it was possible for Wyeth to comply with both federal law and the Vermont-law judgment at issue here. The federal statute and regulations neither prohibited the stronger warning label required by the state judgment, nor insulated Wyeth from the risk of state-law liability. With no "direct conflict" between the federal and state law, then, the state-law judgment is not pre-empted.

The origins of this Court's "purposes and objectives" pre-emption jurisprudence and its broad application illustrate that this brand of the Court's pre-emption jurisprudence facilitates freewheeling, extratextual, and broad evaluations of the "purposes and objectives" embodied within federal law. This, in turn, leads to decisions giving improperly broad pre-emptive effect to judicially manufactured policies, rather than to the statutory text enacted by Congress pursuant to the Constitution and the agency actions authorized thereby. Because such a sweeping approach to pre-emption leads to the illegitimate—and thus, unconstitutional— invalidation of state laws, I can no longer assent to a doctrine that pre-empts state laws merely because they "stan[d] as an obstacle to the accomplishment and execution of the full purposes and objectives" of federal law, as perceived by this Court.

Justice ALITO, with whom the CHIEF JUSTICE and Justice SCALIA join, dissenting.

This case illustrates that tragic facts make bad law. The Court holds that a state tort jury, rather than the Food and Drug Administration (FDA), is ultimately responsible for regulating warning labels for prescription drugs. That result cannot be reconciled with or general principles of conflict pre-emption. I respectfully dissent.

I

The Court frames the question presented as a "narro[w]" one—namely, whether Wyeth has a duty to provide "an adequate warning about using the IV-push method" to administer Phenergan. But that ignores the antecedent question of who—the FDA or a jury in Vermont—has the authority and responsibility for determining the "adequacy" of Phenergan's warnings. Moreover, it is unclear how a "stronger" warning could have helped respondent, after all, the physician's assistant who treated her disregarded at least six separate warnings that are already on Phenergan's labeling, so respondent would be hard pressed to prove that a seventh would have made a difference.

More to the point, the question presented by this case is not a "narrow" one, and it does not concern whether Phenergan's label should bear a "stronger" warning. Rather, the real issue is whether a state tort jury can countermand the FDA's considered judgment that Phenergan's FDA-mandated warning label renders its intravenous (IV) use "safe." Indeed, respondent's amended complaint alleged that Phenergan is "not reasonably safe for intravenous administration." [R]espondent's attorney told the jury that Phenergan's label should say, "Do not use this drug intravenously," respondent's expert told the jury, "I think the drug should be labeled 'Not for IV use,'" and during his closing argument, respondent's attorney told the jury, "Thank God we don't rely on the FDA to ... make the safe[ty] decision. You will make the decision. ... The FDA doesn't make the decision, you do." Federal law, however, *does* rely on the FDA to make safety determinations like the one it made here. The FDA has long known about the risks associated with IV push in general and its use to administer Phenergan in particular. Whether wisely or not, the FDA has concluded—over the course of extensive, 54-year-long regulatory proceedings—that the drug is "safe" and "effective" when used in accordance with its FDA-mandated labeling. The unfortunate fact that respondent's healthcare providers ignored Phenergan's labeling may make this an ideal medical-malpractice case. But turning a common-law tort suit into a "frontal assault" on the FDA's regulatory regime for drug labeling upsets the well-settled meaning of the Supremacy Clause and our conflict pre-emption jurisprudence.

II

To the extent that "[t]he purpose of Congress is the ultimate touchstone in every pre-emption case," Congress made its "purpose" plain in authorizing the FDA—not state tort juries—to determine when and under what circumstances a drug is "safe." Where the FDA determines, in accordance with its statutory mandate, that a drug is on balance "safe," our conflict pre-emption cases prohibit any State from countermanding that determination.

A faithful application of this Court's conflict pre-emption cases compels the conclusion that the FDA's 40-year-long effort to regulate the safety and efficacy of Phenergan pre-empts respondent's tort suit.

Phenergan's warning label has been subject to the FDA's strict regulatory oversight since the 1950's. For at least the last 34 years, the FDA has focused specifically on whether IV-push administration of Phenergan is "safe" and "effective" when performed in accordance with Phenergan's label. The agency's ultimate decision—to retain IV push as one means for administering Phenergan, albeit subject to stringent warnings—is reflected in the plain text of Phenergan's label (sometimes in boldfaced font and all-capital letters). And the record contains ample evidence that the FDA specifically considered and reconsidered the strength of Phenergan's IV-push-related warnings in light of new scientific and medical data. The majority's factual assertions to the contrary are mistaken.

By their very nature, juries are ill-equipped to perform the FDA's cost-benefit-balancing function. [J]uries tend to focus on the risk of a particular product's design or warning label that arguably contributed to a particular plaintiff's injury, not on the overall benefits of that design or label; "the patients who reaped those benefits are not represented in court." Indeed, patients like respondent are the only ones whom tort juries ever see, and for a patient like respondent-who has already suffered a tragic accident—Phenergan's risks are no longer a matter of probabilities and potentialities.

In contrast, the FDA has the benefit of the long view. Its drug-approval determinations consider the interests of all potential users of a drug, including "those who would suffer without new medical [products]" if juries in all 50 States were free to contradict the FDA's expert determinations. And the FDA conveys its warnings with one voice, rather than whipsawing the medical community with 50 (or more) potentially conflicting ones. After today's ruling, however, parochialism may prevail.

To be sure, state tort suits can peacefully coexist with the FDA's labeling regime, and they have done so for decades. But this case is far from peaceful coexistence. The FDA told Wyeth that Phenergan's label renders its use "safe." But the State of Vermont, through its tort law, said: "Not so."

Chapter 8

Fundamental Rights Under Due Process and Equal Protection

L. Procedural Due Process

2. What Procedures Are Required? (casebook, p. 1197)

During October Term 2008, the Court decided two important cases concerning procedural due process. One, *Caperton v. Massey Coal Co.* involved whether due process is violated when a judge has received substantial contributions from a litigant. The other, *District Attorney's Office for the Third Judicial District v. Osborne*, involved whether due process required access to DNA testing for convicted criminal defendants. This case involved both procedural and substantive due process claims. Although the cases arise in very different contexts, they both concern what due process requires.

CAPERTON v. A.T. MASSEY COAL CO., INC.
129 S.Ct. 2252 (2009)

Justice KENNEDY delivered the opinion of the Court.

In this case the Supreme Court of Appeals of West Virginia reversed a trial court judgment, which had entered a jury verdict of $50 million. Five justices heard the case, and the vote to reverse was 3 to 2. The question presented is whether the Due Process Clause of the Fourteenth Amendment was violated when one of the justices in the majority denied a recusal motion. The basis for the motion was that the justice had received campaign contributions in an extraordinary amount from, and through the efforts of, the board chairman and principal officer of the corporation found liable for the damages.

Under our precedents there are objective standards that require recusal when "the probability of actual bias on the part of the judge or decision-maker is too high to be constitutionally tolerable." Applying those

29

precedents, we find that, in all the circumstances of this case, due process requires recusal.

I

In August 2002 a West Virginia jury returned a verdict that found respondents A.T. Massey Coal Co. and its affiliates (hereinafter Massey) liable for fraudulent misrepresentation, concealment, and tortious inter- ference with existing contractual relations. The jury awarded petitioners Hugh Caperton, Harman Development Corp., Harman Mining Corp., and Sovereign Coal Sales (hereinafter Caperton) the sum of $50 million in compensatory and punitive damages.

In June 2004 the state trial court denied Massey's post-trial motions challenging the verdict and the damages award, finding that Massey "intentionally acted in utter disregard of [Caperton's] rights and ultimately destroyed [Caperton's] businesses because, after conducting cost-benefit analyses, [Massey] concluded it was in its financial interest to do so."

Don Blankenship is Massey's chairman, chief executive officer, and president. After the verdict but before the appeal, West Virginia held its 2004 judicial elections. Knowing the Supreme Court of Appeals of West Virginia would consider the appeal in the case, Blankenship decided to support an attorney who sought to replace Justice McGraw. Justice McGraw was a candidate for reelection to that court. The attorney who sought to replace him was Brent Benjamin.

In addition to contributing the $1,000 statutory maximum to Benjamin's campaign committee, Blankenship donated almost $2.5 million to "And For The Sake Of The Kids," a political organization formed under 26 U.S.C. § 527. The § 527 organization opposed McGraw and supported Benjamin. Blankenship's donations accounted for more than two-thirds of the total funds it raised. This was not all. Blankenship spent, in addition, just over $500,000 on independent expenditures—for direct mailings and letters soliciting donations as well as television and news- paper advertisements " 'to support . . . Brent Benjamin.' "

To provide some perspective, Blankenship's $3 million in contribu- tions were more than the total amount spent by all other Benjamin supporters and three times the amount spent by Benjamin's own com- mittee. Caperton contends that Blankenship spent $1 million more than the total amount spent by the campaign committees of both candidates combined.

Benjamin won. He received 382,036 votes (53.3%), and McGraw received 334,301 votes (46.7%).

In October 2005, before Massey filed its petition for appeal in West Virginia's highest court, Caperton moved to disqualify now-Justice Benjamin under the Due Process Clause and the West Virginia Code of Judicial Conduct, based on the conflict caused by Blankenship's campaign involvement. Justice Benjamin denied the motion in April 2006. He indicated that he "carefully considered the bases and accompanying exhibits proffered by the movants." But he found "no objective information . . . to show that this Justice has a bias for or against any litigant, that this Justice has prejudged the matters which comprise this litigation, or that this Justice will be anything but fair and impartial." In December 2006 Massey filed its petition for appeal to challenge the adverse jury verdict. The West Virginia Supreme Court of Appeals granted review.

In November 2007 that court reversed the $50 million verdict against Massey. The majority opinion, authored by then-Chief Justice Davis and joined by Justices Benjamin and Maynard, found that "Massey's conduct warranted the type of judgment rendered in this case." It reversed, nevertheless, based on two independent grounds—first, that a forum-selection clause contained in a contract to which Massey was not a party barred the suit in West Virginia, and, second, that res judicata barred the suit due to an out-of-state judgment to which Massey was not a party.

Caperton sought rehearing, and the parties moved for disqualification of three of the five justices who decided the appeal. Photos had surfaced of Justice Maynard vacationing with Blankenship in the French Riviera while the case was pending. Justice Maynard granted Caperton's recusal motion. On the other side Justice Starcher granted Massey's recusal motion, apparently based on his public criticism of Blankenship's role in the 2004 elections. In his recusal memorandum Justice Starcher urged Justice Benjamin to recuse himself as well. He noted that "Blankenship's bestowal of his personal wealth, political tactics, and 'friendship' have created a cancer in the affairs of this Court." Justice Benjamin declined Justice Starcher's suggestion and denied Caperton's recusal motion.

The court granted rehearing. Justice Benjamin, now in the capacity of acting chief justice, selected Judges Cookman and Fox to replace the recused justices. Caperton moved a third time for disqualification, arguing that Justice Benjamin had failed to apply the correct standard under West Virginia law—*i.e.,* whether "a reasonable and prudent person, knowing these objective facts, would harbor doubts about Justice Benjamin's ability to be fair and impartial." Caperton also included the results of a public opinion poll, which indicated that over 67% of West Virginians doubted Justice Benjamin would be fair and impartial. Justice

Benjamin again refused to withdraw, noting that the "push poll" was "neither credible nor sufficiently reliable to serve as the basis for an elected judge's disqualification."

In April 2008 a divided court again reversed the jury verdict, and again it was a 3-to-2 decision. Justice Davis filed a modified version of her prior opinion, repeating the two earlier holdings. She was joined by Justice Benjamin and Judge Fox. Justice Albright, joined by Judge Cookman, dissented. The dissent also noted "genuine due process implications arising under federal law" with respect to Justice Benjamin's failure to recuse himself.

II

It is axiomatic that "[a] fair trial in a fair tribunal is a basic requirement of due process." As the Court has recognized, however, "most matters relating to judicial disqualification [do] not rise to a constitutional level." The early and leading case on the subject is *Tumey v. Ohio* (1927). There, the Court stated that "matters of kinship, personal bias, state policy, remoteness of interest, would seem generally to be matters merely of legislative discretion."

The *Tumey* Court concluded that the Due Process Clause incorporated the common-law rule that a judge must recuse himself when he has "a direct, personal, substantial, pecuniary interest" in a case. This rule reflects the maxim that "[n]o man is allowed to be a judge in his own cause; because his interest would certainly bias his judgment, and, not improbably, corrupt his integrity." The Federalist No. 10, p. 59 (J. Cooke ed.1961) (J. Madison). Under this rule, "disqualification for bias or prejudice was not permitted"; those matters were left to statutes and judicial codes. Personal bias or prejudice "alone would not be sufficient basis for imposing a constitutional requirement under the Due Process Clause."

As new problems have emerged that were not discussed at common law, however, the Court has identified additional instances which, as an objective matter, require recusal. These are circumstances "in which experience teaches that the probability of actual bias on the part of the judge or decisionmaker is too high to be constitutionally tolerable." To place the present case in proper context, two instances where the Court has required recusal merit further discussion.

The first involved the emergence of local tribunals where a judge had a financial interest in the outcome of a case, although the interest was less than what would have been considered personal or direct at common law. This was the problem addressed in *Tumey*. There, the mayor of a village had the authority to sit as a judge (with no jury) to try those accused of violating a state law prohibiting the possession of alcoholic beverages. Inherent in this structure were two potential conflicts. First, the mayor received a salary supplement for performing judicial duties, and the funds for that compensation derived from the fines assessed in a case. No fines were assessed upon acquittal. The mayor-judge thus received a salary supplement only if he convicted the defendant. Second, sums from the criminal fines were deposited to the village's general treasury fund for village improvements and repairs.

The Court held that the Due Process Clause required disqualification "both because of [the mayor-judge's] direct pecuniary interest in the outcome, and because of his official motive to convict and to graduate the fine to help the financial needs of the village." It so held despite observing that "[t]here are doubtless mayors who would not allow such a consideration as $12 costs in each case to affect their judgment in it." The Court articulated the controlling principle: "Every procedure which would offer a possible temptation to the average man as a judge to forget the burden of proof required to convict the defendant, or which might lead him not to hold the balance nice, clear and true between the State and the accused, denies the latter due process of law."

The Court was thus concerned with more than the traditional common-law prohibition on direct pecuniary interest. It was also concerned with a more general concept of interests that tempt adjudicators to disregard neutrality.

This concern with conflicts resulting from financial incentives was elaborated in *Ward v. Monroeville* (1972), which invalidated a conviction in another mayor's court. In *Monroeville,* unlike in *Tumey,* the mayor received no money; instead, the fines the mayor assessed went to the town's general fisc. The Court held that "[t]he fact that the mayor [in *Tumey*] shared directly in the fees and costs did not define the limits of the principle." The principle, instead, turned on the "possible temptation" the mayor might face; the mayor's "executive responsibilities for village finances may make him partisan to maintain the high level of contribution [to those finances] from the mayor's court."

The second instance requiring recusal that was not discussed at common law emerged in the criminal contempt context, where a judge had no pecuniary interest in the case but was challenged because of a conflict arising from his participation in an earlier proceeding. This Court characterized that first proceeding (perhaps pejoratively) as a " 'one-man grand jury.' "

In that first proceeding, and as provided by state law, a judge examined witnesses to determine whether criminal charges should be brought.

The judge called the two petitioners before him. One petitioner answered questions, but the judge found him untruthful and charged him with perjury. The second declined to answer on the ground that he did not have counsel with him, as state law seemed to permit. The judge charged him with contempt. The judge proceeded to try and convict both petitioners.

This Court set aside the convictions on grounds that the judge had a conflict of interest at the trial stage because of his earlier participation followed by his decision to charge them. The Due Process Clause required disqualification. The Court recited the general rule that "no man can be a judge in his own case," adding that "no man is permitted to try cases where he has an interest in the outcome." It noted that the disqualifying criteria "cannot be defined with precision. Circumstances and relationships must be considered." These circumstances and the prior relationship required recusal: "Having been a part of [the one-man grand jury] process a judge cannot be, in the very nature of things, wholly disinterested in the conviction or acquittal of those accused." That is because "[a]s a practical matter it is difficult if not impossible for a judge to free himself from the influence of what took place in his 'grand-jury' secret session."

III

Based on the principles described in these cases we turn to the issue before us. This problem arises in the context of judicial elections, a framework not presented in the precedents we have reviewed and discussed.

Caperton contends that Blankenship's pivotal role in getting Justice Benjamin elected created a constitutionally intolerable probability of actual bias. Though not a bribe or criminal influence, Justice Benjamin would nevertheless feel a debt of gratitude to Blankenship for his extraordinary efforts to get him elected.

Justice Benjamin was careful to address the recusal motions and explain his reasons why, on his view of the controlling standard, disqualification was not in order. In four separate opinions issued during the course of the appeal, he explained why no actual bias had been established.

Following accepted principles of our legal tradition respecting the proper performance of judicial functions, judges often inquire into their subjective motives and purposes in the ordinary course of deciding a case. This does not mean the inquiry is a simple one. The difficulties of inquiring into actual bias, and the fact that the inquiry is often a private one, simply underscore the need for objective rules. Otherwise there may be no adequate protection against a judge who simply misreads or misapprehends the real motives at work in deciding the case. The judge's own inquiry into actual bias, then, is not one that the law can easily superintend or review, though actual bias, if disclosed, no doubt would be grounds for appropriate relief. In lieu of exclusive reliance on that personal inquiry, or on appellate review of the judge's determination respecting actual bias, the Due Process Clause has been implemented by objective standards that do not require proof of actual bias. In defining these standards the Court has asked whether, "under a realistic appraisal of psychological tendencies and human weakness," the interest "poses such a risk of actual bias or prejudgment that the practice must be forbidden if the guarantee of due process is to be adequately implemented."

We turn to the influence at issue in this case. Not every campaign contribution by a litigant or attorney creates a probability of bias that requires a judge's recusal, but this is an exceptional case. We conclude that there is a serious risk of actual bias—based on objective and reasonable perceptions—when a person with a personal stake in a particular case had a significant and disproportionate influence in placing the judge on the case by raising funds or directing the judge's election campaign when the case was pending or imminent. The inquiry centers on the contribution's relative size in comparison to the total amount of money contributed to the campaign, the total amount spent in the election, and the apparent effect such contribution had on the outcome of the election.

Applying this principle, we conclude that Blankenship's campaign efforts had a significant and disproportionate influence in placing Justice Benjamin on the case. Blankenship contributed some $3 million to unseat the incumbent and replace him with Benjamin. His contributions eclipsed the total amount spent by all other Benjamin supporters and exceeded by 300% the amount spent by Benjamin's campaign committee. Caperton claims Blankenship spent $1 million more than the total amount spent by the campaign committees of both candidates combined.

Massey responds that Blankenship's support, while significant, did not cause Benjamin's victory. In the end the people of West Virginia elected him, and they did so based on many reasons other than Blankenship's efforts. Massey points out that every major state newspaper, but one, endorsed Benjamin. It also contends that then-Justice McGraw cost himself the election by giving a speech during the campaign, a speech the opposition seized upon for its own advantage.

Whether Blankenship's campaign contributions were a necessary and sufficient cause of Benjamin's victory is not the proper inquiry. Much like determining whether a judge is actually biased, proving what ultimately drives the electorate to choose a particular candidate is a difficult endeavor, not likely to lend itself to a certain conclusion. This is particularly true where, as here, there is no procedure for judicial factfinding and the sole trier of fact is the one accused of bias. Due process requires an objective inquiry into whether the contributor's influence on the election under all the circumstances "would offer a possible temptation to the average . . . judge to . . . lead him not to hold the balance nice, clear and true." In an election decided by fewer than 50,000 votes (382,036 to 334,301), Blankenship's campaign contributions—in comparison to the total amount contributed to the campaign, as well as the total amount spent in the election—had a significant and disproportionate influence on the electoral outcome. And the risk that Blankenship's influence engendered actual bias is sufficiently substantial that it "must be forbidden if the guarantee of due process is to be adequately implemented."

The temporal relationship between the campaign contributions, the justice's election, and the pendency of the case is also critical. It was reasonably foreseeable, when the campaign contributions were made, that the pending case would be before the newly elected justice. The $50 million adverse jury verdict had been entered before the election, and the Supreme Court of Appeals was the next step once the state trial court dealt with post-trial motions. So it became at once apparent that, absent recusal, Justice Benjamin would review a judgment that cost his biggest donor's company $50 million. Although there is no allegation of a *quid pro quo* agreement, the fact remains that Blankenship's extraordinary contributions were made at a time when he had a vested stake in the outcome. Just as no man is allowed to be a judge in his own cause, similar fears of bias can arise when—without the consent of the other parties—a man chooses the judge in his own cause. And applying this principle to the judicial election process, there was here a serious, objective risk of actual bias that required Justice Benjamin's recusal.

Justice Benjamin did undertake an extensive search for actual bias. But, as we have indicated, that is just one step in the judicial process; objective standards may also require recusal whether or not actual bias exists or can be proved. Due process "may sometimes bar trial by judges who have no actual bias and who would do their very best to weigh the scales of justice equally between contending parties." The failure to consider objective standards requiring recusal is not consistent with the imperatives of due process. We find that Blankenship's significant and disproportionate influence—coupled with the temporal relationship between the election and the pending case "offer a possible temptation to the average . . . judge to . . . lead him not to hold the balance nice, clear and true." On these extreme facts the probability of actual bias rises to an unconstitutional level.

IV

Our decision today addresses an extraordinary situation where the Constitution requires recusal. Massey and its *amici* predict that various adverse consequences will follow from recognizing a constitutional violation here—ranging from a flood of recusal motions to unnecessary interference with judicial elections. We disagree. The facts now before us are extreme by any measure. The parties point to no other instance involving judicial campaign contributions that presents a potential for bias comparable to the circumstances in this case.

"The Due Process Clause demarks only the outer boundaries of judicial disqualifications. Congress and the states, of course, remain free to impose more rigorous standards for judicial disqualification than those we find mandated here today." Because the codes of judicial conduct provide more protection than due process requires, most disputes over disqualification will be resolved without resort to the Constitution. Application of the constitutional standard implicated in this case will thus be confined to rare instances.

Chief Justice ROBERTS, with whom Justice SCALIA, Justice THOMAS, and Justice ALITO join, dissenting.

I, of course, share the majority's sincere concerns about the need to maintain a fair, independent, and impartial judiciary—and one that appears to be such. But I fear that the Court's decision will undermine rather than promote these values.

Until today, we have recognized exactly two situations in which the Federal Due Process Clause requires disqualification of a judge: when the judge has a financial interest in the outcome of the case, and when the judge is trying a defendant for certain criminal contempts. Vaguer notions of bias or the appearance of bias were never a basis for disqualification, either at common law or under our constitutional precedents. Those issues were instead addressed by legislation or court rules.

Today, however, the Court enlists the Due Process Clause to overturn a judge's failure to recuse because of a "probability of bias." Unlike the established grounds for disqualification, a "probability of bias" cannot be defined in any limited way. The Court's new "rule" provides no guidance to judges and litigants about when recusal will be constitutionally required. This will inevitably lead to an increase in allegations that judges are biased, however groundless those charges may be. The end result will do far more to erode public confidence in judicial impartiality than an isolated failure to recuse in a particular case.

I

There is a "presumption of honesty and integrity in those serving as adjudicators." All judges take an oath to uphold the Constitution and apply the law impartially, and we trust that they will live up to this promise. Subject to the two well-established exceptions described above, questions of judicial recusal are regulated by "common law, statute, or the professional standards of the bench and bar."

In any given case, there are a number of factors that could give rise to a "probability" or "appearance" of bias: friendship with a party or lawyer, prior employment experience, membership in clubs or associations, prior speeches and writings, religious affiliation, and countless other considerations. We have never held that the Due Process Clause requires recusal for any of these reasons, even though they could be viewed as presenting a "probability of bias." Many state *statutes* require recusal based on a probability or appearance of bias, but "that alone would not be sufficient basis for imposing a *constitutional* requirement under the Due Process Clause." States are, of course, free to adopt broader recusal rules than the Constitution requires—and every State has—but these developments are not continuously incorporated into the Due Process Clause.

II

In departing from this clear line between when recusal is constitutionally required and when it is not, the majority repeatedly emphasizes the need for an "objective" standard. The majority's analysis is "objective" in that it does not inquire into Justice Benjamin's motives or decisionmaking process. But the standard the majority articulates—"probability of bias"—fails to provide clear, workable guidance for future cases. At the most basic level, it is unclear whether the new probability of bias standard is somehow limited to financial support in judicial elections, or applies to judicial recusal questions more generally.

But there are other fundamental questions as well. With little help from the majority, courts will now have to determine:

1. How much money is too much money? What level of contribution or expenditure gives rise to a "probability of bias"?

2. How do we determine whether a given expenditure is "disproportionate"? Disproportionate *to what*?

3. Are independent, non-coordinated expenditures treated the same as direct contributions to a candidate's campaign? What about contributions to independent outside groups supporting a candidate?

4. Does it matter whether the litigant has contributed to other candidates or made large expenditures in connection with other elections?

5. Does the amount at issue in the case matter? What if this case were an employment dispute with only $10,000 at stake? What if the plaintiffs only sought non-monetary relief such as an injunction or declaratory judgment?

6. Does the analysis change depending on whether the judge whose disqualification is sought sits on a trial court, appeals court, or state supreme court?

7. How long does the probability of bias last? Does the probability of bias diminish over time as the election recedes? Does it matter whether the judge plans to run for reelection?

8. What if the "disproportionately" large expenditure is made by an industry association, trade union, physicians' group, or the plaintiffs' bar? Must the judge recuse in all cases that affect the association's interests? Must the judge recuse in all cases in which a party or lawyer is a member of that group? Does it matter how much the litigant contributed to the association?

9. What if the case involves a social or ideological issue rather than a financial one? Must a judge recuse from cases involving, say, abortion rights if he has received "disproportionate" support from individuals who feel strongly about either side of that issue? If the supporter wants to help elect judges who are "tough on crime," must the judge recuse in all criminal cases?

10. What if the candidate draws "disproportionate" support from a particular racial, religious, ethnic, or other group, and the case involves an issue of particular importance to that group?

11. What if the supporter is not a party to the pending or imminent case, but his interests will be affected by the decision? Does the Court's analysis apply if the supporter "chooses the judge" not in *his* case, but in someone else's?

12. What if the case implicates a regulatory issue that is of great importance to the party making the expenditures, even though he has no direct financial interest in the outcome (*e.g.,* a facial challenge to an agency rulemaking or a suit seeking to limit an agency's jurisdiction)?

13. Must the judge's vote be outcome determinative in order for his non-recusal to constitute a due process violation?

14. Does the due process analysis consider the underlying merits of the suit? Does it matter whether the decision is clearly right (or wrong) as a matter of state law?

15. What if a lower court decision in favor of the supporter is affirmed on the merits on appeal, by a panel with no "debt of gratitude" to the supporter? Does that "moot" the due process claim?

16. What if the judge voted against the supporter in many other cases?

17. What if the judge disagrees with the supporter's message or tactics? What if the judge expressly *disclaims* the support of this person?

18. Should we assume that elected judges feel a "debt of hostility" towards major *opponents* of their candidacies? Must the judge recuse in cases involving individuals or groups who spent large amounts of money trying unsuccessfully to defeat him?

19. If there is independent review of a judge's recusal decision, *e.g.*, by a panel of other judges, does this completely foreclose a due process claim?

20. Does a debt of gratitude for endorsements by newspapers, interest groups, politicians, or celebrities also give rise to a constitutionally unacceptable probability of bias? How would we measure whether such support is disproportionate?

21. Does close personal friendship between a judge and a party or lawyer now give rise to a probability of bias?

22. Does it matter whether the campaign expenditures come from a party or the party's attorney? If from a lawyer, must the judge recuse in every case involving that attorney?

23. Does what is unconstitutional vary from State to State? What if particular States have a history of expensive judicial elections?

24. Under the majority's "objective" test, do we analyze the due process issue through the lens of a reasonable person, a reasonable lawyer, or a reasonable judge?

25. What role does causation play in this analysis? The Court sends conflicting signals on this point. The majority asserts that "[w]hether Blankenship's campaign contributions were a necessary and sufficient cause of Benjamin's victory is not the proper inquiry." But elsewhere in the opinion, the majority considers "the apparent effect such contribution had on the outcome of the election," and whether the litigant has been able to "choos[e] the judge in his own cause." If causation is a pertinent factor, how do we know whether the contribution or expenditure had any effect on the outcome of the

election? What if the judge won in a landslide? What if the judge won primarily because of his opponent's missteps?

26. Is the due process analysis less probing for incumbent judges—who typically have a great advantage in elections—than for challengers?

27. How final must the pending case be with respect to the contributor's interest? What if, for example, the only issue on appeal is whether the court should certify a class of plaintiffs? Is recusal required just as if the issue in the pending case were ultimate liability?

28. Which cases are implicated by this doctrine? Must the case be pending at the time of the election? Reasonably likely to be brought? What about an important but unanticipated case filed shortly after the election?

29. When do we impute a probability of bias from one party to another? Does a contribution from a corporation get imputed to its executives, and viceversa? Does a contribution or expenditure by one family member get imputed to other family members?

30. What if the election is nonpartisan? What if the election is just a yes-or-no vote about whether to retain an incumbent?

31. What type of support is disqualifying? What if the supporter's expenditures are used to fund voter registration or get-out-the-vote efforts rather than television advertisements?

32. Are contributions or expenditures in connection with a primary aggregated with those in the general election? What if the contributor supported a different candidate in the primary? Does that dilute the debt of gratitude?

33. What procedures must be followed to challenge a state judge's failure to recuse? May *Caperton* claims only be raised on direct review? Or may such claims also be brought in federal district court under 42 U.S.C. § 1983, which allows a person deprived of a federal right by a state official to sue for damages? If § 1983 claims are available, who are the proper defendants? The judge? The whole court? The clerk of court?

34. What about state-court cases that are already closed? Can the losing parties in those cases now seek collateral relief in federal district court under § 1983? What statutes of limitation should be applied to such suits?

35. What is the proper remedy? After a successful *Caperton* motion, must the parties start from scratch before the lower courts? Is any part of the lower court judgment retained?

36. Does a litigant waive his due process claim if he waits until after decision to raise it? Or would the claim only be ripe after decision, when the judge's actions or vote suggest a probability of bias?

37. Are the parties entitled to discovery with respect to the judge's recusal decision?
38. If a judge erroneously fails to recuse, do we apply harmless-error review?
39. Does the *judge* get to respond to the allegation that he is probably biased, or is his reputation solely in the hands of the parties to the case?
40. What if the parties settle a *Caperton* claim as part of a broader settlement of the case? Does that leave the judge with no way to salvage his reputation?

These are only a few uncertainties that quickly come to mind. Judges and litigants will surely encounter others when they are forced to, or wish to, apply the majority's decision in different circumstances. Today's opinion requires state and federal judges simultaneously to act as political scientists (why did candidate X win the election?), economists (was the financial support disproportionate?), and psychologists (is there likely to be a debt of gratitude?).

The Court's inability to formulate a "judicially discernible and manageable standard" strongly counsels against the recognition of a novel constitutional right.

III

To its credit, the Court seems to recognize that the inherently boundless nature of its new rule poses a problem. But the majority's only answer is that the present case is an "extreme" one, so there is no need to worry about other cases.

But this is just so much whistling past the graveyard. Claims that have little chance of success are nonetheless frequently filed. The success rate for certiorari petitions before this Court is approximately 1.1%, and yet the previous Term some 8,241 were filed. Every one of the "*Caperton* motions" or appeals or § 1983 actions will claim that the judge is biased, or probably biased, bringing the judge and the judicial system into disrepute. And all future litigants will assert that their case is *really* the most extreme thus far.

Extreme cases often test the bounds of established legal principles. There is a cost to yielding to the desire to correct the extreme case, rather than adhering to the legal principle. That cost has been demonstrated so often that it is captured in a legal aphorism: "Hard cases make bad law."

The déjà vu is enough to make one swoon. Today, the majority again departs from a clear, longstanding constitutional rule to accommodate an "extreme" case involving "grossly disproportionate" amounts of money. I believe we will come to regret this decision as well, when courts are forced to deal with a wide variety of *Caperton* motions, each claiming the title of "most extreme" or "most disproportionate."

B

And why is the Court so convinced that this is an extreme case? It is true that Don Blankenship spent a large amount of money in connection with this election. But this point cannot be emphasized strongly enough: Other than a $1,000 direct contribution from Blankenship, *Justice Benjamin and his campaign had no control over how this money was spent.* Campaigns go to great lengths to develop precise messages and strategies. An insensitive or ham-handed ad campaign by an independent third party might distort the campaign's message or cause a backlash against the candidate, even though the candidate was not responsible for the ads.

Moreover, Blankenship's independent expenditures do not appear "grossly disproportionate" compared to other such expenditures in this very election. "And for the Sake of the Kids"—an independent group that received approximately two-thirds of its funding from Blankenship—spent $3,623,500 in connection with the election. But large independent expenditures were also made in support of Justice Benjamin's opponent. "Consumers for Justice"—an independent group that received large contributions from the plaintiffs' bar—spent approximately $2 million in this race. And Blankenship has made large expenditures in connection with several previous West Virginia elections, which undercuts any notion that his involvement in this election was "intended to influence the outcome" of particular pending litigation.

It is also far from clear that Blankenship's expenditures affected the outcome of this election. Justice Benjamin won by a comfortable 7-point margin (53.3% to 46.7%). Many observers believed that Justice Benjamin's opponent doomed his candidacy by giving a well-publicized speech that made several curious allegations; this speech was described in the local media as "deeply disturbing" and worse. Justice Benjamin's opponent also refused to give interviews or participate in debates. All but one of the major West Virginia newspapers endorsed Justice Benjamin. Justice Benjamin just might have won because the voters of West Virginia thought he would be a better judge than his opponent. Unlike the majority, I cannot say with any degree of certainty that Blankenship "cho[se] the judge in his own cause." I would give the voters of West Virginia more credit than that.

It is an old cliché, but sometimes the cure is worse than the disease. I am sure there are cases where a "probability of bias" should lead the prudent judge to step aside, but the judge fails to do so. Maybe this is one of them. But I believe that opening the door to recusal claims under the Due Process Clause, for an amorphous "probability of bias," will itself bring our judicial system into undeserved disrepute, and diminish the confidence of the American people in the fairness and integrity of their courts. I hope I am wrong. . . .

DISTRICT ATTORNEY'S OFFICE FOR THE THIRD JUDICIAL DISTRICT v. OSBORNE
129 S.Ct. 2308 (2009)

Chief Justice ROBERTS delivered the opinion of the Court.

DNA testing has an unparalleled ability both to exonerate the wrongly convicted and to identify the guilty. It has the potential to significantly improve both the criminal justice system and police investigative practices. The Federal Government and the States have recognized this, and have developed special approaches to ensure that this evidentiary tool can be effectively incorporated into established criminal procedure— usually but not always through legislation.

Against this prompt and considered response, the respondent, William Osborne, proposes a different approach: the recognition of a freestanding and far-reaching constitutional right of access to this new type of evidence. This approach would take the development of rules and procedures in this area out of the hands of legislatures and state courts shaping policy in a focused manner and turn it over to federal courts applying the broad parameters of the Due Process Clause. There is no reason to constitutionalize the issue in this way. Because the decision below would do just that, we reverse.

I

This lawsuit arose out of a violent crime committed 16 years ago, which has resulted in a long string of litigation in the state and federal courts. On the evening of March 22, 1993, two men driving through Anchorage, Alaska, solicited sex from a female prostitute, K.G. She agreed to perform fellatio on both men for $100 and got in their car. The three spent some time looking for a place to stop and ended up in a deserted area near Earthquake Park. When K.G. demanded payment in advance, the two men pulled out a gun and forced her to perform fellatio on the driver while the passenger penetrated her vaginally, using a blue condom she had brought. The passenger then ordered K.G. out of the car and told her to lie face-down in the snow. Fearing for her life, she refused, and the two men choked her and beat her with the gun. When K.G. tried to flee, the passenger beat her with a wooden axe handle and shot her in the head while she lay on the ground. They kicked some snow on top of her and left her for dead.

K.G. did not die; the bullet had only grazed her head. Once the two men left, she found her way back to the road, and flagged down a passing car to take her home. Ultimately, she received medical care and spoke to the police. At the scene of the crime, the police recovered a spent shell casing, the axe handle, some of K.G.'s clothing stained with blood, and the blue condom.

Six days later, two military police officers at Fort Richardson pulled over Dexter Jackson for flashing his headlights at another vehicle. In his car they discovered a gun (which matched the shell casing), as well as several items K.G. had been carrying the night of the attack. The car also matched the description K.G. had given to the police. Jackson admitted that he had been the driver during the rape and assault, and told the police that William Osborne had been his passenger. Other evidence also implicated Osborne. K.G. picked out his photograph (with some uncertainty) and at trial she identified Osborne as her attacker. Other witnesses testified that shortly before the crime, Osborne had called Jackson from an arcade, and then driven off with him. An axe handle similar to the one at the scene of the crime was found in Osborne's room on the military base where he lived.

The State also performed DQ Alpha testing on sperm found in the blue condom. DQ Alpha testing is a relatively inexact form of DNA testing that can clear some wrongly accused individuals, but generally cannot narrow the perpetrator down to less than 5% of the population. The semen found on the condom had a genotype that matched a blood sample taken from Osborne, but not ones from Jackson, K. G., or a third suspect named James Hunter. Osborne is black, and approximately 16% of black individuals have such a genotype. App. 117-119. In other words, the testing ruled out Jackson and Hunter as possible sources of the semen, and also ruled out over 80% of other black individuals. The State also examined some pubic hairs found at the scene of the crime, which were not susceptible to DQ Alpha testing, but which state witnesses attested to be similar to Osborne's.

Osborne and Jackson were convicted by an Alaska jury of kidnapping, assault, and sexual assault. They were acquitted of an additional count of sexual assault and of attempted murder. Finding it "nearly miraculous" that K.G. had survived, the trial judge sentenced Osborne to 26 years in prison, with 5 suspended. His conviction and sentence were affirmed on appeal. Osborne then sought postconviction relief in Alaska state court. He claimed that he had asked his attorney, Sidney Billingslea, to seek more discriminating restriction-fragment-length-polymorphism (RFLP) DNA testing during trial, and argued that she was constitutionally ineffective for not doing so. In two decisions, the Alaska Court of Appeals concluded that Osborne had no right to the RFLP test. The court relied heavily on the fact that Osborne had confessed to some of his crimes in a 2004 application for parole—in which it is a crime to lie. In this statement, Osborne acknowledged forcing K.G. to have sex at gunpoint, as well as beating her and covering her with snow. He repeated this confession before the parole board.

II

Modern DNA testing can provide powerful new evidence unlike anything known before. Since its first use in criminal investigations in the mid-1980s, there have been several major advances in DNA technology, culminating in STR technology. It is now often possible to determine whether a biological tissue matches a suspect with near certainty. While of course many criminal trials proceed without any forensic and scientific testing at all, there is no technology comparable to DNA testing for matching tissues when such evidence is at issue. DNA testing has exonerated wrongly convicted people, and has confirmed the convictions of many others.

At the same time, DNA testing alone does not always resolve a case. Where there is enough other incriminating evidence and an explanation for the DNA result, science alone cannot prove a prisoner innocent. The availability of technologies not available at trial cannot mean that every criminal conviction, or even every criminal conviction involving biological evidence, is suddenly in doubt. The dilemma is how to harness DNA's power to prove innocence without unnecessarily overthrowing the established system of criminal justice.

That task belongs primarily to the legislature. "[T]he States are currently engaged in serious, thoughtful examinations," of how to ensure the fair and effective use of this testing within the existing criminal justice framework. Forty-six States have already enacted statutes dealing specifically with access to DNA evidence. The State of Alaska itself is considering joining them. The Federal Government has also passed the Innocence Protection Act of 2004, which allows federal prisoners to move for court-ordered DNA testing under certain specified conditions.

These laws recognize the value of DNA evidence but also the need for certain conditions on access to the State's evidence. A requirement of demonstrating materiality is common, but it is not the only one. The federal statute, for example, requires a sworn statement that the applicant is innocent. This requirement is replicated in several state statutes. States also impose a range of diligence requirements. Several require the requested testing to "have been technologically impossible at trial." Others deny testing to those who declined testing at trial for tactical reasons.

Alaska is one of a handful of States yet to enact legislation specifically addressing the issue of evidence requested for DNA testing. But that does not mean that such evidence is unavailable for those seeking to prove their innocence. Instead, Alaska courts are addressing how to apply existing laws for discovery and postconviction relief to this novel technology. [T]he Alaska Court of Appeals has invoked a widely accepted three-part test to govern additional rights to DNA access under the State Constitution. Drawing on the experience with DNA evidence of State Supreme Courts around the country, the Court of Appeals explained that it was "reluctant to hold that Alaska law offers no remedy to defendants who could prove their factual innocence." It was "prepared to hold, however, that a defendant who seeks post-conviction DNA testing . . . must show (1) that the conviction rested primarily on eyewitness identification evidence, (2) that there was a demonstrable doubt concerning the defendant's identification as the perpetrator, and (3) that scientific testing would likely be conclusive on this issue." Thus, the Alaska courts have suggested that even those who do not get discovery under the State's criminal rules have available to them a safety valve under the State Constitution.

[III]

"No State shall . . . deprive any person of life, liberty, or property, without due process of law." This Clause imposes procedural limitations on a State's power to take away protected entitlements. Osborne argues that access to the State's evidence is a "process" needed to vindicate his right to prove himself innocent and get out of jail. Process is not an end in itself, so a necessary premise of this argument is that he has an entitlement (what our precedents call a "liberty interest") to prove his innocence even after a fair trial has proved otherwise. We must first examine this asserted liberty interest to determine what process (if any) is due.

In identifying his potential liberty interest, Osborne first attempts to rely on the Governor's constitutional authority to "grant pardons, commutations, and reprieves." That claim can be readily disposed of. We have held that noncapital defendants do not have a liberty interest in traditional state executive clemency, to which no particular claimant is *entitled* as a matter of state law. Osborne therefore cannot challenge the constitutionality of any procedures available to vindicate an interest in state clemency.

Osborne does, however, have a liberty interest in demonstrating his innocence with new evidence under state law. As explained, Alaska law provides that those who use "newly discovered evidence" to "establis[h] by clear and convincing evidence that [they are] innocent" may obtain "vacation of [their] conviction or sentence in the interest of justice." This "state-created right can, in some circumstances, beget yet other rights to procedures essential to the realization of the parent right."

A criminal defendant proved guilty after a fair trial does not have the same liberty interests as a free man. At trial, the defendant is presumed innocent and may demand that the government prove its case beyond reasonable doubt. But "[o]nce a defendant has been afforded a fair trial and convicted of the offense for which he was charged, the presumption of innocence disappears." "Given a valid conviction, the criminal defendant has been constitutionally deprived of his liberty."

The State accordingly has more flexibility in deciding what procedures are needed in the context of postconviction relief. "[W]hen a State chooses to offer help to those seeking relief from convictions," due process does not "dictat[e] the exact form such assistance must assume." Osborne's right to due process is not parallel to a trial right, but rather must be analyzed in light of the fact that he has already been found guilty at a fair trial, and has only a limited interest in postconviction relief. *Brady* is the wrong framework.

Instead, the question is whether consideration of Osborne's claim within the framework of the State's procedures for postconviction relief "offends some principle of justice so rooted in the traditions and conscience of our people as to be ranked as fundamental," or "transgresses any recognized principle of fundamental fairness in operation."

We see nothing inadequate about the procedures Alaska has provided to vindicate its state right to postconviction relief in general, and nothing inadequate about how those procedures apply to those who seek access to DNA evidence. Alaska provides a substantive right to be released on a sufficiently compelling showing of new evidence that establishes innocence. It exempts such claims from otherwise applicable time limits. The

State provides for discovery in postconviction proceedings, and has—through judicial decision—specified that this discovery procedure is available to those seeking access to DNA evidence. These procedures are not without limits. The evidence must indeed be newly available to qualify under Alaska's statute, must have been diligently pursued, and must also be sufficiently material. These procedures are similar to those provided for DNA evidence by federal law and the law of other States and they are not inconsistent with the "traditions and conscience of our people" or with "any recognized principle of fundamental fairness." And there is more. While the Alaska courts have not had occasion to conclusively decide the question, the Alaska Court of Appeals has suggested that the State Constitution provides an additional right of access to DNA. In expressing its "reluctan[ce] to hold that Alaska law offers no remedy" to those who belatedly seek DNA testing, and in invoking the three-part test used by other state courts, the court indicated that in an appropriate case the State Constitution may provide a failsafe even for those who cannot satisfy the statutory requirements under general postconviction procedures.

The Court of Appeals below relied only on procedural due process, but Osborne seeks to defend the judgment on the basis of substantive due process as well. He asks that we recognize a freestanding right to DNA evidence untethered from the liberty interests he hopes to vindicate with it. We reject the invitation and conclude, in the circumstances of this case, that there is no such substantive due process right. "As a general matter, the Court has always been reluctant to expand the concept of substantive due process because guideposts for responsible decision-making in this unchartered area are scarce and open-ended." Osborne seeks access to state evidence so that he can apply new DNA-testing technology that might prove him innocent. There is no long history of such a right, and "[t]he mere novelty of such a claim is reason enough to doubt that 'substantive due process' sustains it."

And there are further reasons to doubt. The elected governments of the States are actively confronting the challenges DNA technology poses to our criminal justice systems and our traditional notions of finality, as well as the opportunities it affords. To suddenly constitutionalize this area would short-circuit what looks to be a prompt and considered legislative response. The first DNA testing statutes were passed in 1994 and 1997. In the past decade, 44 States and the Federal Government have followed suit, reflecting the increased availability of DNA testing. As noted, Alaska itself is considering such legislation. "By extending constitutional protection to an asserted right or liberty interest, we, to a great extent, place the matter outside the arena of public debate and legislative action. We must therefore exercise the utmost care whenever we are asked to break new ground in this field." "[J]udicial imposition of a categorical remedy ... might pretermit other responsible solutions being considered in Congress and state legislatures." If we extended substantive due process to this area, we would cast these statutes into constitutional doubt and be forced to take over the issue of DNA access ourselves. We are reluctant to enlist the Federal Judiciary in creating a new constitutional code of rules for handling DNA.

Establishing a freestanding right to access DNA evidence for testing would force us to act as policymakers, and our substantive-due-process rulemaking authority would not only have to cover the right of access but a myriad of other issues. We would soon have to decide if there is a constitutional obligation to preserve forensic evidence that might later be tested. If so, for how long? Would it be different for different types of evidence? Would the State also have some obligation to gather such evidence in the first place? How much, and when? No doubt there would be a miscellany of other minor directives.

DNA evidence will undoubtedly lead to changes in the criminal justice system. It has done so already. The question is whether further change will primarily be made by legislative revision and judicial inter-pretation of the existing system, or whether the Federal Judiciary must leap ahead—revising (or even discarding) the system by creating a new constitutional right and taking over responsibility for refining it.

Federal courts should not presume that state criminal procedures will be inadequate to deal with technological change. The criminal justice system has historically accommodated new types of evidence, and is a time-tested means of carrying out society's interest in convicting the guilty while respecting individual rights. That system, like any human endeavor, cannot be perfect. DNA evidence shows that it has not been. But there is no basis for Osborne's approach of assuming that because DNA has shown that these procedures are not flawless, DNA evidence must be treated as categorically outside the process, rather than within it.

Justice STEVENS, with whom Justice GINSBURG and Justice BREYER join, and with whom Justice SOUTER joins as to Part I, dissenting.

The State of Alaska possesses physical evidence that, if tested, will conclusively establish whether respondent William Osborne committed rape and attempted murder. If he did, justice has been served by his conviction and sentence. If not, Osborne has needlessly spent decades behind bars while the true culprit has not been brought to justice. The

DNA test Osborne seeks is a simple one, its cost modest, and its results uniquely precise. Yet for reasons the State has been unable or unwilling to articulate, it refuses to allow Osborne to test the evidence at his own expense and to thereby ascertain the truth once and for all.

Because I am convinced that Osborne has a constitutional right of access to the evidence he wishes to test and that, on the facts of this case, he has made a sufficient showing of entitlement to that evidence, I would affirm the decision of the Court of Appeals.

Osborne asserts a right to access the State's evidence that derives from the Due Process Clause itself. Whether framed as a "substantive liberty interest . . . protected through a procedural due process right" to have evidence made available for testing, or as a substantive due process right to be free of arbitrary government action, the result is the same: On the record now before us, Osborne has established his entitlement to test the State's evidence.

The liberty protected by the Due Process Clause is not a creation of the Bill of Rights. Indeed, our Nation has long recognized that the liberty safeguarded by the Constitution has far deeper roots.

Although a valid criminal conviction justifies punitive detention, it does not entirely eliminate the liberty interests of convicted persons. For while a prisoner's "rights may be diminished by the needs and exigencies of the institutional environment[,] . . . [t]here is no iron curtain drawn between the Constitution and the prisons of this country." It is therefore far too late in the day to question the basic proposition that convicted persons such as Osborne retain a constitutionally protected measure of interest in liberty, including the fundamental liberty of freedom from physical restraint.

Recognition of this right draws strength from the fact that 46 States and the Federal Government have passed statutes providing access to evidence for DNA testing, and 3 additional states (including Alaska) provide similar access through court-made rules alone.These legislative developments are consistent with recent trends in legal ethics recognizing that prosecutors are obliged to disclose all forms of exculpatory evidence that come into their possession following conviction. The fact that nearly all the States have now recognized some postconviction right to DNA evidence makes it more, not less, appropriate to recognize a limited federal right to such evidence in cases where litigants are unfairly barred from obtaining relief in state court.

Recent scientific advances in DNA analysis have made "it literally possible to confirm guilt or innocence beyond any question whatsoever, at least in some categories of cases." As the Court recognizes today, the powerful new evidence that modern DNA testing can provide is "unlike anything known before."

If the right Osborne seeks to vindicate is framed as purely substantive, the proper result is no less clear. "The touchstone of due process is protection of the individual against arbitrary action of government." When government action is so lacking in justification that it "can properly be characterized as arbitrary, or conscience shocking, in a constitutional sense," it violates the Due Process Clause. In my view, the State's refusal to provide Osborne with access to evidence for DNA testing qualifies as arbitrary.

Throughout the course of state and federal litigation, the State has failed to provide any concrete reason for denying Osborne the DNA testing he seeks, and none is apparent. Because Osborne has offered to pay for the tests, cost is not a factor. And as the State now concedes, there is no reason to doubt that such testing would provide conclusive confirmation of Osborne's guilt or revelation of his innocence. In the courts below, the State refused to provide an explanation for its refusal to permit testing of the evidence, and in this Court, its explanation has been, at best, unclear. Insofar as the State has articulated any reason at all, it appears to be a generalized interest in protecting the finality of the judgment of conviction from any possible future attacks.

While we have long recognized that States have an interest in securing the finality of their judgments, finality is not a stand-alone value that trumps a State's overriding interest in ensuring that justice is done in its courts and secured to its citizens. Indeed, when absolute proof of innocence is readily at hand, a State should not shrink from the possibility that error may have occurred. Rather, our system of justice is strengthened by "recogniz[ing] the need for, and imperative of, a safety valve in those rare instances where objective proof that the convicted actually did not commit the offense later becomes available through the progress of science."

This conclusion draws strength from the powerful state interests that offset the State's purported interest in finality *per se*. When a person is convicted for a crime he did not commit, the true culprit escapes punishment. DNA testing may lead to his identification. Crime victims, the law enforcement profession, and society at large share a strong interest in identifying and apprehending the actual perpetrators of vicious crimes, such as the rape and attempted murder that gave rise to this case.

The arbitrariness of the State's conduct is highlighted by comparison to the private interests it denies. It seems to me obvious that if a wrongly convicted person were to produce proof of his actual innocence, no state interest would be sufficient to justify his continued punitive detention. If such proof can be readily obtained without imposing a significant burden on the State, a refusal to provide access to such evidence is wholly unjustified.

In sum, an individual's interest in his physical liberty is one of constitutional significance. That interest would be vindicated by providing postconviction access to DNA evidence, as would the State's interest in ensuring that it punishes the true perpetrator of a crime. In this case, the State has suggested no countervailing interest that justifies its refusal to allow Osborne to test the evidence in its possession and has not provided any other nonarbitrary explanation for its conduct. Consequently, I am left to conclude that the State's failure to provide Osborne access to the evidence constitutes arbitrary action that offends basic principles of due process.

Chapter 9

First Amendment: Freedom of Expression

B. Free Speech Methodology

1. The Distinction Between Content-Based and Content-Neutral Laws

c. Problems in Applying the Distinction Between Content-Based and Content-Neutral Laws (casebook, p. 1232)

In *Pleasant Grove City, Utah v. Summum*, the Supreme Court held that the government may engage in content-based discrimination when the government is the speaker. The Court held this in the context of the government adopting a privately donated monument as its own speech. The question will be whether this will open the door to the government engaging in content-based discrimination by adopting other private speech as government expression.

PLEASANT GROVE CITY, UTAH v. SUMMUM
129 S.Ct. 1125 (2009)

Justice ALITO delivered the opinion of the Court.

This case presents the question whether the Free Speech Clause of the First Amendment entitles a private group to insist that a municipality permit it to place a permanent monument in a city park in which other donated monuments were previously erected. The Court of Appeals held that the municipality was required to accept the monument because a public park is a traditional public forum. We conclude, however, that although a park is a traditional public forum for speeches and other transitory expressive acts, the display of a permanent monument in a public park is not a form of expression to which forum analysis applies.

Instead, the placement of a permanent monument in a public park is best viewed as a form of government speech and is therefore not subject to scrutiny under the Free Speech Clause.

I

Pioneer Park (or Park) is a 2.5 acre public park located in the Historic District of Pleasant Grove City (or City) in Utah. The Park currently contains 15 permanent displays, at least 11 of which were donated by private groups or individuals. These include an historic granary, a wishing well, the City's first fire station, a September 11 monument, and a Ten Commandments monument donated by the Fraternal Order of Eagles in 1971.

Respondent Summum is a religious organization founded in 1975 and headquartered in Salt Lake City, Utah. On two separate occasions in 2003, Summum's president wrote a letter to the City's mayor requesting permission to erect a "stone monument," which would contain "the Seven Aphorisms of SUMMUM" and be similar in size and nature to the Ten Commandments monument. The City denied the requests.

In May 2005, respondent's president again wrote to the mayor asking to erect a monument, but the letter did not describe the monument, its historical significance, or Summum's connection to the community. The city council rejected this request.

In 2005, respondent filed this action against the City and various local officials (petitioners), asserting, among other claims, that petitioners had violated the Free Speech Clause of the First Amendment by accepting the Ten Commandments monument but rejecting the proposed Seven Aphorisms monument.

II

No prior decision of this Court has addressed the application of the Free Speech Clause to a government entity's acceptance of privately donated, permanent monuments for installation in a public park, and the parties disagree sharply about the line of precedents that governs this situation. The parties' fundamental disagreement thus centers on the nature of petitioners' conduct when they permitted privately donated monuments to be erected in Pioneer Park. Were petitioners engaging in their own expressive conduct? Or were they providing a forum for private speech?

If petitioners were engaging in their own expressive conduct, then the Free Speech Clause has no application. The Free Speech Clause restricts government regulation of private speech; it does not regulate government speech. Indeed, it is not easy to imagine how government could function if it lacked this freedom. "If every citizen were to have a right to insist that no one paid by public funds express a view with which he disagreed, debate over issues of great concern to the public would be limited to those in the private sector, and the process of government as we know it radically transformed."

A government entity may exercise this same freedom to express its views when it receives assistance from private sources for the purpose of delivering a government-controlled message.

This does not mean that there are no restraints on government speech. For example, government speech must comport with the Establishment Clause. The involvement of public officials in advocacy may be limited by law, regulation, or practice. And of course, a government entity is ultimately "accountable to the electorate and the political process for its advocacy."

While government speech is not restricted by the Free Speech Clause, the government does not have a free hand to regulate private speech on government property. This Court long ago recognized that members of the public retain strong free speech rights when they venture into public streets and parks, "which 'have immemorially been held in trust for the use of the public and, time out of mind, have been used for purposes of assembly, communicating thoughts between citizens, and discussing public questions.'" In order to preserve this freedom, government entities are strictly limited in their ability to regulate private speech in such "traditional public fora." Reasonable time, place, and manner restrictions are allowed, but any restriction based on the content of the speech must satisfy strict scrutiny, that is, the restriction must be narrowly tailored to serve a compelling government interest, and restrictions based on viewpoint are prohibited.

III

There may be situations in which it is difficult to tell whether a government entity is speaking on its own behalf or is providing a forum for private speech, but this case does not present such a situation. Permanent monuments displayed on public property typically represent government speech.

Governments have long used monuments to speak to the public. Since ancient times, kings, emperors, and other rulers have erected statues of themselves to remind their subjects of their authority and power. Triumphal arches, columns, and other monuments have been built to commemorate military victories and sacrifices and other events of civic importance. A monument, by definition, is a structure that is designed as a means of expression. When a government entity arranges for the construction of a monument, it does so because it wishes to convey some thought or instill some feeling in those who see the structure. Neither the Court of Appeals nor respondent disputes the obvious proposition that a monument that is commissioned and financed by a government body for placement on public land constitutes government speech.

Just as government-commissioned and government-financed monuments speak for the government, so do privately financed and donated monuments that the government accepts and displays to the public on government land. It certainly is not common for property owners to open up their property for the installation of permanent monuments that convey a message with which they do not wish to be associated. And because property owners typically do not permit the construction of such monuments on their land, persons who observe donated monuments routinely—and reasonably—interpret them as conveying some message on the property owner's behalf. In this context, there is little chance that observers will fail to appreciate the identity of the speaker. This is true whether the monument is located on private property or on public property, such as national, state, or city park land.

Public parks are often closely identified in the public mind with the government unit that owns the land. City parks ranging from those in small towns, like Pioneer Park in Pleasant Grove City, to those in major metropolises, like Central Park in New York City—commonly play an important role in defining the identity that a city projects to its own residents and to the outside world. Accordingly, cities and other jurisdictions take some care in accepting donated monuments. Government decisionmakers select the monuments that portray what they view as appropriate for the place in question, taking into account such content-based factors as esthetics, history, and local culture. The monuments that are accepted, therefore, are meant to convey and have the effect of conveying a government message, and they thus constitute government speech.

IV

In this case, it is clear that the monuments in Pleasant Grove's Pioneer Park represent government speech. Although many of the monuments were not designed or built by the City and were donated in completed form by private entities, the City decided to accept those donations and to display them in the Park. Respondent does not claim that the City ever opened up the Park for the placement of whatever permanent monuments might be offered by private donors. Rather, the City has "effectively controlled" the messages sent by the monuments in the Park by exercising "final approval authority" over their selection. The City has selected those monuments that it wants to display for the purpose of presenting the image of the City that it wishes to project to all who frequent the Park; it has taken ownership of most of the monuments in the Park, including the Ten Commandments monument that is the focus of respondent's concern; and the City has now expressly set forth the criteria it will use in making future selections.

Respondent voices the legitimate concern that the government speech doctrine not be used as a subterfuge for favoring certain private speakers over others based on viewpoint. Respondent's suggested solution is to require a government entity accepting a privately donated monument to go through a formal process of adopting a resolution publicly embracing "the message" that the monument conveys.

We see no reason for imposing a requirement of this sort. The parks of this country contain thousands of donated monuments that government entities have used for their own expressive purposes, usually without producing the sort of formal documentation that respondent now says is required to escape Free Speech Clause restrictions. Requiring all of these jurisdictions to go back and proclaim formally that they adopt all of these monuments as their own expressive vehicles would be a pointless exercise that the Constitution does not mandate.

Contrary to respondent's apparent belief, it frequently is not possible to identify a single "message" that is conveyed by an object or structure, and consequently, the thoughts or sentiments expressed by a government entity that accepts and displays such an object may be quite different from those of either its creator or its donor. By accepting a privately donated monument and placing it on city property, a city engages in expressive conduct, but the intended and perceived significance of that conduct may not coincide with the thinking of the monument's donor or creator. Indeed, when a privately donated memorial is funded by many small donations, the donors themselves may differ in their interpretation of the monument's significance. By accepting such a monument, a government entity does not necessarily endorse the specific meaning that any particular donor sees in the monument.

Respondent and the Court of Appeals analogize the installation of permanent monuments in a public park to the delivery of speeches and the holding of marches and demonstrations, and they thus invoke the rule that a public park is a traditional public forum for these activities. But "public forum principles . . . are out of place in the context of this case." The forum doctrine has been applied in situations in which government-owned property or a government program was capable of accommodating a large number of public speakers without defeating the essential function of the land or the program. For example, a park can accommodate many speakers and, over time, many parades and demonstrations.

By contrast, public parks can accommodate only a limited number of permanent monuments. Public parks have been used, " 'time out of mind, . . . for purposes of assembly, communicating thoughts between citizens, and discussing public questions,' " but "one would be hard pressed to find a 'long tradition' of allowing people to permanently occupy public space with any manner of monuments."

Speakers, no matter how long-winded, eventually come to the end of their remarks; persons distributing leaflets and carrying signs at some point tire and go home; monuments, however, endure. They monopolize the use of the land on which they stand and interfere permanently with other uses of public space. A public park, over the years, can provide a soapbox for a very large number of orators—often, for all who want to speak—but it is hard to imagine how a public park could be opened up for the installation of permanent monuments by every person or group wishing to engage in that form of expression.

If government entities must maintain viewpoint neutrality in their selection of donated monuments, they must either "brace themselves for an influx of clutter" or face the pressure to remove longstanding and cherished monuments. Every jurisdiction that has accepted a donated war memorial may be asked to provide equal treatment for a donated monument questioning the cause for which the veterans fought. New York City, having accepted a donated statue of one heroic dog (Balto, the sled dog who brought medicine to Nome, Alaska, during a diphtheria epidemic) may be pressed to accept monuments for other dogs who are claimed to be equally worthy of commemoration. The obvious truth of the matter is that if public parks were considered to be traditional public forums for the purpose of erecting privately donated monuments, most parks would have little choice but to refuse all such donations. And where the application of forum analysis would lead almost inexorably to closing of the forum, it is obvious that forum analysis is out of place.

To be sure, there are limited circumstances in which the forum doctrine might properly be applied to a permanent monument—for example, if a town created a monument on which all of its residents (or all those meeting some other criterion) could place the name of a person to be honored or some other private message. But as a general matter, forum analysis simply does not apply to the installation of permanent monuments on public property.

V

In sum, we hold that the City's decision to accept certain privately donated monuments while rejecting respondent's is best viewed as a form of government speech. As a result, the City's decision is not subject to the Free Speech Clause, and the Court of Appeals erred in holding otherwise. We therefore reverse.

Justice STEVENS, with whom Justice GINSBURG joins, concurring.

This case involves a property owner's rejection of an offer to place a permanent display on its land. While I join the Court's persuasive opinion, I think the reasons justifying the city's refusal would have been equally valid if its acceptance of the monument, instead of being characterized as "government speech," had merely been deemed an implicit endorsement of the donor's message. To date, our decisions relying on the recently minted government speech doctrine to uphold government action have been few and, in my view, of doubtful merit. The Court's opinion in this case signals no expansion of that doctrine. And by joining the Court's opinion, I do not mean to indicate agreement with our earlier decisions. Nor is it likely, given the near certainty that observers will associate permanent displays with the governmental property owner, that the government will be able to avoid political accountability for the views that it endorses or expresses through this means. Finally, recognizing permanent displays on public property as government speech will not give the government free license to communicate offensive or partisan messages. For even if the Free Speech Clause neither restricts nor protects government speech, government speakers are bound by the Constitution's other proscriptions, including those supplied by the Establishment and Equal Protection Clauses. Together with the checks imposed by our democratic processes, these constitutional safeguards ensure that the effect of today's decision will be limited.

Justice SCALIA, with whom Justice THOMAS joins, concurring.

As framed and argued by the parties, this case presents a question under the Free Speech Clause of the First Amendment. I agree with the

Court's analysis of that question and join its opinion in full. But it is also obvious that from the start, the case has been litigated in the shadow of the First Amendment's *Establishment* Clause: the city wary of associating itself too closely with the Ten Commandments monument displayed in the park, lest that be deemed a breach in the so-called "wall of separation between church and State."

The city ought not fear that today's victory has propelled it from the Free Speech Clause frying pan into the Establishment Clause fire. Contrary to respondent's intimations, there are very good reasons to be confident that the park displays do not violate *any* part of the First Amendment.

In *Van Orden v. Perry* (2005), this Court upheld against Establishment Clause challenge a virtually identical Ten Commandments monument, donated by the very same organization (the Fraternal Order of Eagles), which was displayed on the grounds surrounding the Texas State Capitol. Nothing in that decision suggested that the outcome turned on a finding that the monument was only "private" speech.

The city can safely exhale. Its residents and visitors can now return to enjoying Pioneer Park's wishing well, its historic granary—and, yes, even its Ten Commandments monument—without fear that they are complicit in an establishment of religion.

Justice BREYER, concurring.

I agree with the Court and join its opinion. I do so, however, on the understanding that the "government speech" doctrine is a rule of thumb, not a rigid category. Were the City to discriminate in the selection of permanent monuments on grounds unrelated to the display's theme, say solely on political grounds, its action might well violate the First Amendment.

In my view, courts must apply categories such as "government speech," "public forums," "limited public forums," and "nonpublic forums" with an eye towards their purposes—lest we turn "free speech" doctrine into a jurisprudence of labels. Consequently, we must sometimes look beyond an initial categorization. And, in doing so, it helps to ask whether a government action burdens speech disproportionately in light of the action's tendency to further a legitimate government objective.

Were we to do so here, we would find—for reasons that the Court sets forth—that the City's action, while preventing Summum from erecting its monument, does not disproportionately restrict Summum's freedom of expression. The City has not closed off its parks to speech; no one claims that the City prevents Summum's members from engaging in speech in a form more transient than a permanent monument. Rather, the City has simply reserved some space in the park for projects designed to further other than free-speech goals. And that is perfectly proper. After all, parks do not serve speech-related interests alone. To the contrary, cities use park space to further a variety of recreational, historical, educational, aesthetic, and other civic interests. To reserve to the City the power to pick and choose among proposed monuments according to criteria reasonably related to one or more of these legitimate ends restricts Summum's expression, but, given the impracticality of alternatives and viewed in light of the City's legitimate needs, the restriction is not disproportionate. Analyzed either way, as "government speech" or as a proportionate restriction on Summum's expression, the City's action here is lawful.

Justice SOUTER, concurring in the judgment.

I agree with the Court that the Ten Commandments monument is government speech, that is, an expression of a government's position on the moral and religious issues raised by the subject of the monument. And although the government should lose when the character of the speech is at issue and its governmental nature has not been made clear, I also agree with the Court that the city need not satisfy the particular formality urged by Summum as a condition of recognizing that the expression here falls within the public category. I have qualms, however, about accepting the position that public monuments are government speech categorically.

Because the government speech doctrine is "recently minted," it would do well for us to go slow in setting its bounds, which will affect existing doctrine in ways not yet explored.

The case shows that it may not be easy to work out. After today's decision, whenever a government maintains a monument it will presumably be understood to be engaging in government speech. If the monument has some religious character, the specter of violating the Establishment Clause will behoove it to take care to avoid the appearance of a flat-out establishment of religion, in the sense of the government's adoption of the tenets expressed or symbolized. In such an instance, there will be safety in numbers, and it will be in the interest of a careful government to accept other monuments to stand nearby, to dilute the appearance of adopting whatever particular religious position the single example alone might stand for. As mementoes and testimonials pile up, however, the chatter may well make it less intuitively obvious that the government is speaking in its own right simply by maintaining the monuments.

To avoid relying on a *per se* rule to say when speech is governmental, the best approach that occurs to me is to ask whether a reasonable and fully informed observer would understand the expression to be government speech, as distinct from private speech the government chooses to oblige by allowing the monument to be placed on public land. This reasonable observer test for governmental character is of a piece with the one for spotting forbidden governmental endorsement of religion in the Establishment Clause cases. The adoption of it would thus serve coherence within Establishment Clause law, and it would make sense of our common understanding that some monuments on public land display religious symbolism that clearly does not express a government's chosen views.

Application of this observer test provides the reason I find the monument here to be government expression.

C. *Types of Unprotected and Less Protected Speech*

3. Sexually Oriented Speech

i. *The Broadcast Media (casebook page. 1412)*

In *FCC v. Pacifica Foundation* (casebook p. 1412), the Supreme Court held that television and radio broadcasters could be punished for indecent speech. The Court did not deal, though, with a single use of a profanity (the so-called 'fleeting expletive'). In 2004, the Federal Communication Commission changed its policy so that it would punish single uses of profanities. The United States Court of Appeals for the Second Circuit invalidated this, concluding that it was an arbitrary agency action in violation of the Administrative Procedures Act. The Supreme Court reversed in a 5-4 decision. Justice Scalia's majority opinion focused entirely on the Administrative Procedures Act and did not decide the First Amendment question. But several of the other opinions do address the First Amendment issue.

FEDERAL COMMUNICATIONS COMMISSION, et al. v. FOX TELEVISION STATIONS, INC., et al.
128 S.Ct. 1800 (2009)

JUSTICE SCALIA delivered the opinion of the Court, except as to Part III-E.

Federal law prohibits the broadcasting of "any . . . indecent . . . language," which includes expletives referring to sexual or excretory activity or organs. This case concerns the adequacy of the Federal Communications Commission's explanation of its decision that this sometimes forbids the broadcasting of indecent expletives even when the offensive words are not repeated.

I. Statutory and Regulatory Background

The Communications Act of 1934, established a system of limited-term broadcast licenses subject to various "conditions" designed "to maintain the control of the United States over all the channels of radio transmission." Twenty-seven years ago we said that "[a] licensed broadcaster is granted the free and exclusive use of a limited and valuable part of the public domain; when he accepts that franchise it is burdened by enforceable public obligations."

One of the burdens that licensees shoulder is the indecency ban— the statutory proscription against "utter[ing] any obscene, indecent, or profane language by means of radio communication." Congress has instructed the Commission to enforce between the hours of 6AM and 10PM. Congress has given the Commission various means of enforcing the indecency ban, including civil fines, and license revocations or the denial of license renewals.

The Commission first invoked the statutory ban on indecent broadcasts in 1975, declaring a daytime broadcast of George Carlin's "Filthy Words" monologue actionably indecent. In *FCC v. Pacifica Foundation,* we upheld the Commission's order against statutory and constitutional challenge. We rejected the broadcasters' argument that the statutory proscription applied only to speech appealing to the prurient interest, noting that "the normal definition of 'indecent' merely refers to non-conformance with accepted standards of morality." And we held that the First Amendment allowed Carlin's monologue to be banned in light of the "uniquely pervasive presence" of the medium and the fact that broadcast programming is "uniquely accessible to children."

In the ensuing years, the Commission took a cautious, but gradually expanding, approach to enforcing the statutory prohibition against indecent broadcasts. Shortly after the Commission expressed its "inten[tion] strictly to observe the narrowness of the *Pacifica* holding," which "relied in part on the repetitive occurrence of the 'indecent' words" contained in Carlin's monologue. When the full Commission next considered its indecency standard, however, it repudiated the view that its enforcement power was limited to "deliberate, repetitive use of the seven words actually contained in the George Carlin monologue." The Commission determined that such a "highly restricted enforcement standard . . . was unduly narrow as a matter of law and inconsistent with [the Commission's] enforcement responsibilities under Section 1464."

Although the Commission had expanded its enforcement beyond the "repetitive use of specific words or phrases," it preserved a distinction between literal and nonliteral (or "expletive") uses of evocative language. The Commission explained that each literal "description or depiction of sexual or excretory functions must be examined in context to determine whether it is patently offensive," but that "deliberate and repetitive use . . . is a requisite to a finding of indecency" when a complaint focuses solely on the use of nonliteral expletives.

In 2004, the Commission took one step further by declaring for the first time that a nonliteral (expletive) use of the F- and S-Words could be actionably indecent, even when the word is used only once. The first order to this effect dealt with an NBC broadcast of the Golden Globe Awards, in which the performer Bono commented, "'This is really, really, f***ing brilliant.'" Although the Commission had received numerous complaints directed at the broadcast, its enforcement bureau had concluded that the material was not indecent because "Bono did not describe, in context, sexual or excretory organs or activities and . . . the utterance was fleeting and isolated." The full Commission reviewed and reversed the staff ruling.

The Commission first declared that Bono's use of the F-Word fell within its indecency definition, even though the word was used as an intensifier rather than a literal descriptor. "[G]iven the core meaning of the 'F-Word,'" it said, "any use of that word . . . inherently has a sexual connotation." The Commission determined, moreover, that the broadcast was "patently offensive" because the F-Word "is one of the most vulgar, graphic and explicit descriptions of sexual activity in the English language," because "[i]ts use invariably invokes a coarse sexual image," and because Bono's use of the word was entirely "shocking and gratuitous."

The Commission observed that categorically exempting such language from enforcement actions would "likely lead to more widespread use." Commission action was necessary to "safeguard the well-being of the nation's children from the most objectionable, most offensive language." The order noted that technological advances have made it far easier to delete ("bleep out") a "single and gratuitous use of a vulgar expletive," without adulterating the content of a broadcast.

The order acknowledged that "prior Commission and staff action have indicated that isolated or fleeting broadcasts of the 'F-Word' . . . are not indecent or would not be acted upon." It explicitly ruled that "any such interpretation is no longer good law." It "clarif[ied] . . . that the mere fact that specific words or phrases are not sustained or repeated does not mandate a finding that material that is otherwise patently offensive to the broadcast medium is not indecent." Because, however, "existing precedent would have permitted this broadcast," the Commission determined that "NBC and its affiliates necessarily did not have the requisite notice to justify a penalty."

II. The Present Case

This case concerns utterances in two live broadcasts aired by Fox Television Stations, Inc., and its affiliates prior to the Commission's *Golden Globes Order*. The first occurred during the 2002 Billboard Music Awards, when the singer Cher exclaimed, "I've also had critics for the last 40 years saying that I was on my way out every year. Right. So f*** 'em." The second involved a segment of the 2003 Billboard Music Awards, during the presentation of an award by Nicole Richie and Paris Hilton, principals in a Fox television series called "The Simple Life." Ms. Hilton began their interchange by reminding Ms. Richie to "watch the bad language," but Ms. Richie proceeded to ask the audience, "Why do they even call it 'The Simple Life?' Have you ever tried to get cow s*** out of a Prada purse? It's not so f***ing simple." Following each of these broadcasts, the Commission received numerous complaints from parents whose children were exposed to the language.

On March 15, 2006, the Commission released Notices of Apparent Liability for a number of broadcasts that the Commission deemed actionably indecent, including the two described above. Multiple parties petitioned the Court of Appeals for the Second Circuit for judicial review of the order, asserting a variety of constitutional and statutory challenges.

The order first explained that both broadcasts fell comfortably within the subject-matter scope of the Commission's indecency test because the

2003 broadcast involved a literal description of excrement and both broadcasts invoked the "F-Word," which inherently has a sexual connotation. The order next determined that the broadcasts were patently offensive under community standards for the medium. Both broadcasts, it noted, involved entirely gratuitous uses of "one of the most vulgar, graphic, and explicit words for sexual activity in the English language." It found Ms. Richie's use of the "F-Word" and her "explicit description of the handling of excrement" to be "vulgar and shocking," as well as to constitute "pandering," after Ms. Hilton had playfully warned her to "'watch the bad language.'" And it found Cher's statement patently offensive in part because she metaphorically suggested a sexual act as a means of expressing hostility to her critics. The order relied upon the "critically important" context of the utterances, noting that they were aired during prime-time awards shows "designed to draw a large nationwide audience that could be expected to include many children interested in seeing their favorite music stars." Indeed, approximately 2.5 million minors witnessed each of the broadcasts.

Fox returned to the Second Circuit for review of the *Remand Order*, and various intervenors including CBS, NBC, and ABC joined the action. The Court of Appeals reversed the agency's orders, finding the Commission's reasoning inadequate under the Administrative Procedure Act.

III. Analysis

A. Governing Principles

The Administrative Procedure Act, 5 U.S.C. § 551 *et seq.*, which sets forth the full extent of judicial authority to review executive agency action for procedural correctness, permits (insofar as relevant here) the setting aside of agency action that is "arbitrary" or "capricious." Under what we have called this "narrow" standard of review, we insist that an agency "examine the relevant data and articulate a satisfactory explanation for its action." We have made clear, however, that "a court is not to substitute its judgment for that of the agency," and should "uphold a decision of less than ideal clarity if the agency's path may reasonably be discerned."

We find no basis in the Administrative Procedure Act or in our opinions for a requirement that all agency change be subjected to more searching review. The Act mentions no such heightened standard.

To be sure, the requirement that an agency provide reasoned explanation for its action would ordinarily demand that it display awareness that it *is* changing position. In this appeal from the Second Circuit's setting aside of Commission action for failure to comply with a procedural requirement of the Administrative Procedure Act, the broadcasters' arguments have repeatedly referred to the First Amendment. If they mean to invite us to apply a more stringent arbitrary-and-capricious review to agency actions that implicate constitutional liberties, we reject the invitation. The so-called canon of constitutional avoidance is an interpretive tool, counseling that ambiguous statutory language be construed to avoid serious constitutional doubts. We know of no precedent for applying it to limit the scope of authorized executive action. In the same section authorizing courts to set aside "arbitrary [or] capricious" agency action, the Administrative Procedure Act separately provides for setting aside agency action that is "unlawful," which of course includes unconstitutional action. We think that is the only context in which constitutionality bears upon judicial review of authorized agency action. If the Commission's action here was not arbitrary or capricious in the ordinary sense, it satisfies the Administrative Procedure Act's "arbitrary [or] capricious" standard; its lawfulness under the Constitution is a separate question to be addressed in a constitutional challenge.

B. Application to This Case

Judged under the above described standards, the Commission's new enforcement policy and its order finding the broadcasts actionably indecent were neither arbitrary nor capricious. First, the Commission forthrightly acknowledged that its recent actions have broken new ground, taking account of inconsistent "prior Commission and staff action" and explicitly disavowing them as "no longer good law." Moreover, the agency's reasons for expanding the scope of its enforcement activity were entirely rational. It was certainly reasonable to determine that it made no sense to distinguish between literal and nonliteral uses of offensive words, requiring repetitive use to render only the latter indecent. As the Commission said with regard to expletive use of the F-Word, "the word's power to insult and offend derives from its sexual meaning." And the Commission's decision to look at the patent offensiveness of even isolated uses of sexual and excretory words fits with the context-based approach we sanctioned in. Even isolated utterances can be made in "pander[ing,] . . . vulgar and shocking" manners, and can constitute harmful "'first blow[s]'" to children. It is surely rational (if not inescapable) to believe that a safe harbor for single words would "likely lead to more widespread use of the offensive language."

The fact that technological advances have made it easier for broadcasters to bleep out offending words further supports the Commission's stepped-up enforcement policy. And the agency's decision not to impose any forfeiture or other sanction precludes any argument that it is arbitrarily punishing parties without notice of the potential consequences of their action.

IV. Constitutionality

The Second Circuit did not definitively rule on the constitutionality of the Commission's orders, but respondents nonetheless ask us to decide their validity under the First Amendment. This Court, however, is one of final review, "not of first view." It is conceivable that the Commission's orders may cause some broadcasters to avoid certain language that is beyond the Commission's reach under the Constitution. Whether that is so, and, if so, whether it is unconstitutional, will be determined soon enough, perhaps in this very case. Meanwhile, any chilled references to excretory and sexual material "surely lie at the periphery of First Amendment concern." We see no reason to abandon our usual procedures in a rush to judgment without a lower court opinion. We decline to address the constitutional questions at this time. . . .

The Second Circuit believed that children today "likely hear this language far more often from other sources than they did in the 1970's when the Commission first began sanctioning indecent speech," and that this cuts against more stringent regulation of broadcasts. Assuming the premise is true (for this point the Second Circuit did not demand empirical evidence) the conclusion does not necessarily follow. The Commission could reasonably conclude that the pervasiveness of foul language, and the coarsening of public entertainment in other media such as cable, justify more stringent regulation of broadcast programs so as to give conscientious parents a relatively safe haven for their children. In the end, the Second Circuit and the broadcasters quibble with the Commission's policy choices and not with the explanation it has given. We decline to "substitute [our] judgment for that of the agency," and we find the Commission's orders neither arbitrary nor capricious.

JUSTICE THOMAS, concurring.

I join the Court's opinion, which, as a matter of administrative law, correctly upholds the Federal Communications Commission's (FCC) policy with respect to indecent broadcast speech under the Administrative Procedure Act. I write separately, however, to note the questionable viability of the two precedents that support the FCC's assertion of constitutional authority to regulate the programming at issue in this case. See *Red Lion Broadcasting Co. v. FCC* (1969); *FCC v. Pacifica Foundation* (1978). *Red Lion* and *Pacifica* were unconvincing when they were issued, and the passage of time has only increased doubt regarding their continued validity. "The text of the First Amendment makes no distinctions among print, broadcast, and cable media, but we have done so" in these cases.

Highlighting the doctrinal incoherence of *Red Lion* and *Pacifica,* the Court has declined to apply the lesser standard of First Amendment scrutiny imposed on broadcast speech to federal regulation of telephone dial-in services, see *Sable Communications of Cal., Inc. v. FCC* (1989), cable television programming, see *Turner Broadcasting System, Inc. v. FCC* (1994), and the Internet, see *Reno v. American Civil Liberties Union* (1997). "There is no justification for this apparent dichotomy in First Amendment jurisprudence. Whatever the merits of *Pacifica* when it was issued [,] . . . it makes no sense now." The justifications relied on by the Court in *Red Lion* and *Pacifica*—"spectrum scarcity, intrusiveness, and accessibility to children—neither distinguish broadcast from cable, nor explain the relaxed application of the principles of the First Amendment to broadcast."

Second, even if this Court's disfavored treatment of broadcasters under the First Amendment could have been justified at the time of *Red Lion* and *Pacifica,* dramatic technological advances have eviscerated the factual assumptions underlying those decisions. Broadcast spectrum is significantly less scarce than it was 40 years ago. As NBC notes, the number of over-the-air broadcast stations grew from 7,411 in 1969, when *Red Lion* was issued, to 15,273 by the end of 2004. And the trend should continue with broadcast television's imminent switch from analog to digital transmission, which will allow the FCC to "stack broadcast channels right beside one another along the spectrum, and ultimately utilize significantly less than the 400 MHz of spectrum the analog system absorbs today."

Moreover, traditional broadcast television and radio are no longer the "uniquely pervasive" media forms they once were. For most consumers, traditional broadcast media programming is now bundled with cable or satellite services. Broadcast and other video programming is also widely available over the Internet. And like radio and television broadcasts, Internet access is now often freely available over the airwaves and can be accessed by portable computer, cell phones, and other wireless devices. The extant facts that drove this Court to subject broadcasters to unique disfavor under the First Amendment simply do not exist today.

These dramatic changes in factual circumstances might well support a departure from precedent under the prevailing approach to *stare decisis*. For all these reasons, I am open to reconsideration of *Red Lion* and *Pacifica* in the proper case.

JUSTICE STEVENS, dissenting.

While I join JUSTICE BREYER's cogent dissent, I think it important to emphasize two flaws in the Court's reasoning. Apparently assuming that the Federal Communications Commission's (FCC or Commission) rule-making authority is a species of executive power, the Court espouses the novel proposition that the Commission need not explain its decision to discard a longstanding rule in favor of a dramatically different approach to regulation. Moreover, the Court incorrectly assumes that our decision in *FCC v. Pacifica Foundation* (1978), decided that the word "indecent," as used in 18 U.S.C. § 1464, permits the FCC to punish the broadcast of *any* expletive that has a sexual or excretory origin. *Pacifica* was not so sweeping, and the Commission's changed view of its statutory mandate certainly would have been rejected if presented to the Court at the time.

The Court commits a second critical error by assuming that *Pacifica* endorsed a construction of the term "indecent," as used in 18 U.S.C. § 1464, that would include any expletive that has a sexual or excretory origin. Neither the opinion of the Court, nor Justice Powell's concurring opinion, adopted such a far-reaching interpretation. Our holding was narrow in two critical respects. First, we concluded, over the dissent of four Justices, that the statutory term "indecent" was not limited to material that had prurient appeal and instead included material that was in "nonconformance with accepted standards of morality." Second, we upheld the FCC's adjudication that a 12-minute, expletive-filled monologue by satiric humorist George Carlin was indecent "as broadcast." We did not decide whether an *isolated* expletive could qualify as indecent. And we certainly did not hold that any word with a sexual or scatological origin, however used, was indecent.

The narrow treatment of the term "indecent" in *Pacifica* defined the outer boundaries of the enforcement policies adopted by the FCC in the ensuing years.[1] Even if the words that concern the Court in this case *sometimes* retain their sexual or excretory meaning, there are surely countless instances in which they are used in a manner unrelated to their origin. These words may not be polite, but that does not mean they are necessarily "indecent" under § 1464. By improperly equating the two, the Commission has adopted an interpretation of "indecency" that bears no resemblance to what *Pacifica* contemplated. Most distressingly, the Commission appears to be entirely unaware of this fact. Because the FCC has failed to demonstrate an awareness that it has ventured far beyond *Pacifica*'s reading of § 1464, its policy choice must be declared arbitrary and set aside as unlawful.

JUSTICE GINSBURG, dissenting.

I write separately only to note that there is no way to hide the long shadow the First Amendment casts over what the Commission has done. Today's decision does nothing to diminish that shadow.

More than 30 years ago, a sharply divided Court allowed the FCC to sanction a midafternoon radio broadcast of comedian George Carlin's 12-minute "Filthy Words" monologue.

In contrast, the unscripted fleeting expletives at issue here are neither deliberate nor relentlessly repetitive. Nor does the Commission's policy home in on expressions used to describe sexual or excretory activities or organs. Spontaneous utterances used simply to convey an emotion or intensify a statement fall within the order's compass.

The *Pacifica* decision, however it might fare on reassessment was tightly cabined, and for good reason. In dissent, JUSTICE BRENNAN observed that the Government should take care before enjoining the broadcast of words or expressions spoken by many "in our land of cultural pluralism." That comment, fitting in the 1970's, is even more potent today. If the reserved constitutional question reaches this Court, we should be mindful that words unpalatable to some may be "commonplace" for others, "the stuff of everyday conversations."

JUSTICE BREYER, with whom JUSTICE STEVENS, JUSTICE SOUTER, and JUSTICE GINSBURG join, dissenting.

In my view, the Federal Communications Commission failed adequately to explain *why* it *changed* its indecency policy from a policy permitting a single "fleeting use" of an expletive, to a policy that made no such exception. Its explanation fails to discuss two critical factors,

---

1. It is ironic, to say the least, that while the FCC patrols the airwaves for words that have a tenuous relationship with sex or excrement, commercials broadcast during prime-time hours frequently ask viewers whether they too are battling erectile dysfunction or are having trouble going to the bathroom. [Footnote by Justice Stevens]

at least one of which directly underlay its original policy decision. Its explanation instead discussed several factors well known to it the first time around, which by themselves provide no significant justification for a *change* of policy. Consequently, the FCC decision is "arbitrary, capricious, an abuse of discretion."